CW01150500

MANTRAS
FOR SUCCESS

MANTRAS FOR SUCCESS

INDIA'S GREATEST CEOs TELL YOU HOW TO WIN

SUHEL SETH

with SUNNY SEN

MAVEN
RUPA

Published in Maven by
Rupa Publications India Pvt. Ltd 2015
7/16, Ansari Road, Daryaganj
New Delhi 110002

Sales Centres:
Allahabad Bengaluru Chennai
Hyderabad Jaipur Kathmandu
Kolkata Mumbai

Copyright © Suhel Seth 2015

All rights reserved.
No part of this publication may be reproduced, transmitted,
or stored in a retrieval system, in any form or by any means,
electronic, mechanical, photocopying, recording or otherwise,
without the prior permission of the publisher.

The views and opinions expressed in this book are the author's own and the facts are as reported by him/her which have been verified to the extent possible, and the publishers are not in any way liable for the same.

ISBN: 978-81-291-3567-4

First impression 2015

10 9 8 7 6 5 4 3 2 1

The moral right of the author has been asserted.

Printed by Thomson Press India Ltd, Faridabad.

This book is sold subject to the condition that it shall not,
by way of trade or otherwise, be lent, resold, hired out,
or otherwise circulated, without the publisher's prior consent, in any
form of binding or cover other than that in which it is published.

CONTENTS

Introduction   1
Suhel Seth

The Change Architect   21
Ratan Tata

The Unstoppable Magnate   33
Mukesh Ambani

The God of Big Things   45
Anand Mahindra

The Takeover Titan   59
Kumar Mangalam Birla

The Changeover Man   71
Adi Godrej

A Phone-man's Legacy   83
Sunil Bharti Mittal

The Story of Two Bankers   95
Deepak Parekh and Aditya Puri

The House of Mr Biyani   107
Kishore Biyani

The Real Hero *Pawan Munjal*	119
The Compulsive Entrepreneur *Analjit Singh*	131
The Healer *Kiran Mazumdar-Shaw*	143
The Era of a Hotelier *P.R.S. Oberoi*	155
Walking in His Own Shadow *Sanjiv Goenka*	167
The Man who Created Gurgaon *K.P. Singh*	177
Sky Isn't the Limit *Naresh Goyal*	189
The Online Maverick *Kunal Bahl*	199
Maximizing Success *Rahul Sharma*	211
The Disciple *Rajiv Memani*	223
The Perfect Take-off *Aditya Ghosh*	235
Getting the Fizz Back *Atul Singh*	247
Acknowledgements *Sunny Sen*	261

INTRODUCTION

I firmly believe lists are deviously deceptive, for several reasons. They are lists, and not some obtuse narrative, so they are limited. They are almost always supported by substantive findings, call it research or accolades or whatever. They always leave some delighted and others disgusted. But lists help people remember. They are great chroniclers of both the past and the present. The easy thing for me to do here would have been to rely on some research agency to make a list and then publish the results, which would be akin to the many lists we see every year.

But this book is not a list of profiles of business leaders. It is not based on balance sheets and annual reports. I did not want you, the reader, to read a tome or, for that matter, reams and reams of jargon. This book is about India's greatest CEOs and the things that make them great. It is about their souls—their personal convictions and their styles of management. It is about the way they see their companies in the context of both consumers and communities. These mantras are a blend of their emotional and rational beliefs and the decisions that they took. These are not just management mantras; these are life mantras. It shows the reader how CEOs morph from being good to being great.

This is not an arbitrary list. These people have been selected after going through reams of business stories over the last fifteen years, which have talked about India's best in business and lauded their leadership.

The pages ahead capture the mantras of these great doyens of Indian business, who have undoubtedly left a mark on their global counterparts. Their mantras have been woven deftly into their achievements. We have attempted to highlight the impact that their mantras have had in real life. They are not just quotable quotes but, in fact, the soul of their business ideas.

For me, this book was important for two main reasons. First, there isn't a single book out there that brings the thoughts of the greatest Indian corporate leaders together. Second, many of those who are featured in this book have maintained a stoic silence about their working lives so far, and this was one way people could gain an insight into their working styles and beliefs, and through them, into the world of doing business in India. What is it that drives these CEOs to be audacious whilst being so deeply rooted in what they do? Why do they sometimes take decisions fraught with risks that most men and women would shy away from?

I have stayed away from writing a pure-play marketing book because of the flux inherent in the exercise. As the consumer changes with the passage of every nano-second, so must marketing. This constant movement will not easily lend itself to a book.

Mantras for Success is about India's greatest CEOs. It does not include CEOs of Indian origin or, for that matter, Indians who are CEOs elsewhere in the world or foreigners who are CEOs of Indian companies. The reason for this is that there is something unique about being an Indian CEO in India. Indian CEOs have to navigate many minefields before even thinking of reaching the consumer. And once they do, the vagaries of doing business in India are so challenging that it takes a lot of courage, at times guile, perhaps even foresight, to get on with what they wish to achieve. Being a CEO in India today, with an overzealous media, is not easy. Indian businesspersons have also been criticized for being part of a system that is prone to crony capitalism. They have lived and worked under the shadow of suspicion, where every attempt has been made to denigrate their achievements. Therefore, the first task while working on this book was to highlight those who have built businesses that have inspired people.

Then there is the social cost that a leader incurs. India and Indians don't take too easily to failure. We consider failure as a sign of inherent foolishness or the inability to read things right. We don't believe that someone we admire is capable of failure and yet, when that person fails, we almost revel in his or her downfall. One of the biggest highlights of the book is the mantra that success can't be achieved without failure. Being audacious in business is an enduring virtue and I won't even bother amplifying the cliché that if you dare to dream, half the battle is won. But that is just a saying, and cannot always be true. The role of hindsight is always brought out in books such as these but I have carefully stayed away from this rather romantic notion of doing business. Hindsight is a good essay subject but not when you are examining the life and times of CEOs operating in the real world with real-time problems.

Choosing the CEOs was tough and to write about them was tougher. Sunny Sen did months of rigorous research and burnt the midnight oil night after night to put this together. His excellent work in providing the backgrounds and then setting the mantras in their rightful context needs to be lauded. He has provided the window through which you see the worlds these leaders inhabit and the roles they play.

Of the greats profiled in this book, some inherited their company but left their own indelible imprints on it. Mukesh Ambani, for example, inherited a business empire, but what he did to Reliance was transformational. He moved Reliance from an oil and gas corporation to a conglomerate, which straddles telecom and retail along with its core businesses.

I have known Mukesh for almost two decades. In every interaction with him, I have come away with two main thoughts about the man: he is a passionate Indian and he is an avowed believer in the Indian Dream. When you have people like him helming large corporations, you come away believing rather than just admiring.

Mukesh, through his mantras, suggests that scale of a business alone is not enough; vision is nothing if not passed through the prism of implementation and consumer connect. It is this juxtaposition that we need to examine.

Even in the mantras that Mukesh has penned for this book, you will see an unflinching zeal for scale and a huge belief in the Make-in-India proposition, which is now the birthmark of our current prime minister Narendra Modi's vision for India Inc. Similarly, Anand Mahindra, Pawan Munjal and Ratan Tata, among others, also firmly believe in the India story.

Ratan Tata strode the corporate world like a colossus. He is one man who epitomizes the credo that values are more important than valuations. The House of Tata is no ordinary business house, and Bombay House is no ordinary corporate office. Ratan, whom I have known for a decade, was studying in the US and had landed a job at International Business Machines (IBM). He happened to come to India to see his ailing grandfather, and soon found himself drawn into the family business. Over the years he built the House of Tata into one of India's powerhouses of business, which went all over the world.

But the name Tata is associated with more than just business. Ratan has always stood out not just for his stubborn risk-taking but for his foresight, which includes a heavy dose of passion. I have never seen him passionless, be it anything he does, whether it is renewing his pilot's license at Le Bourget every year or, for that matter, his spartan style.

The Tata group has always done business with an eye towards the community. They inject a dose of ethics into everything they do. But more than anything else, they have always believed that nation-building and adding value to the Indian fabric is the purpose of their work. When Ratan took over the company, he was not just battling business issues in a liberalizing India. He was also waging a war with certain group CEOs who had become titular heads of the businesses they were running. This was the House of Tata then, which had many tenants attempting to define its architecture, who misconstrued Ratan's lack of age for lack of wisdom. In the many years that I have known Ratan, the one mistake you never make is to believe you know him well.

Ratan is perhaps the most adept at combining consistency with the art of surprise. He brought those skills to work when he took over the House of Tata. He knew where to intervene and where to stay away and, as I mentioned, wherever he intervened, it was with a mix of business imperatives and unbridled passion. He used a simple solution for the most complex of challenges and every business in the House of Tata began to bear the identity of a family, rather than warring factions who would come together only to feast. He brought in accountability where there were powerful people accountable to no one, not even their stakeholders.

It is this simplicity that Ratan Tata captures so evocatively in his mantras for this book. It is not easy to extract mantras from him. He is a firm believer that your deeds should speak for themselves; he does not believe in spouting preachy quotes. Ratan invigorated a plodding conglomerate and inspired a moribund House of Tata to take global strides. And every stride he took had unflinching attention to detail and was part of a grand plan that perhaps only he knew.

What began as global conquests with the Tetleys of the world spread to categories such as steel and automobiles. Everyone smirked when he bid for (and acquired) Jaguar and Land Rover. But very few people knew that Ratan would not just win the bid, he would also win over consumers since he is and has always been passionate about cars. His fund of knowledge came not just from copious research but also from the gut. So while the House of Tata was making global forays, back in India, Ratan began building the ethics quotient of the group. Cyrus P. Mistry, the current chairman, has actually created the office of a chief ethics officer in Tata.

CEOs love to wage wars when their principles and their policies are sound. Moving the Tata Nano project out of Singur in West Bengal, to Sanand in Gujarat, was a reflection of Ratan's overpowering belief in the organization and his ability to chart a course that would ordinarily defy logic. Logic is for statistics. Not for great leaders.

In the ultimate analysis, Ratan Tata's contributions to India may have been through the prism of business but they will eventually be hailed as coming more out of the basic human values that he has never strayed from. He was an entrepreneur in a house that had already been built. He actually changed the company without altering its edifice. Obviously, his degree in architecture from Cornell must have come in handy.

I can go on and on, but there are many more equals in this book.

Sunil Bharti Mittal became the face of Indian telecom in the late 1990s. He used his skills of business management and entrepreneurship, honed in the small town of Ludhiana in

India's predominantly agricultural state of Punjab, to build Airtel. Being Punjabi helped—Punjabis often take risks without even realizing it. The garrulous effervescence of the average Punjabi easily spills over to business, as Sunil has shown time and again.

I have known Sunil for the longest time, from when Airtel was not even one-fourth of what it is today. He remains loyal to his friends, he is extremely wily (as he should be) and he has mastered the ability to be politically neutral, which means he can do business regardless of political ups and downs. Like most CEOs, he has had to buffer many storms. He has shown not just courage but the belief that these are passing tempests that may wreck his short-term plans but will never impact the long term. Which is why, in his mantras, there is an element of steadfastness that shines through as his personal belief statement. His company is young and nimble on its feet. He symbolizes recent Indian success. Courage and conviction will always remain his twin halos.

The other key ingredient captured in the mantras that Sunil has espoused is a high degree of trust, not just in his colleagues but equally in his partners. When he outsourced his entire technology management to IBM, people scoffed. But Sunil, more than anyone else, knew that technology was regenerative so why would he take on that capital expenditure? He also understood very quickly that he was in the conversation business and only flawless technology would guarantee consumer delight.

Then there is Kumar Mangalam Birla. Personally, he is perhaps not in direct competition with Sunil, but his telecom company, Idea Cellular, is. Started as a company consisting of three partners, the other two being Tata and AT&T, Kumar Mangalam made it one cohesive unit by buying out the other two. He then got the right people to run the business and made it the third-largest telecom operator in the country. But then Kumar Mangalam is not focused only on one business. He has spread himself across sectors from manufacturing and retail to natural resources and agriculture. For Kumar Mangalam, like Mukesh Ambani, scale is very important. He does not want to be in businesses where his group will not be in the top three.

If Sunil is the face of Indian telecom, Pawan Munjal of Hero MotoCorp is synonymous with motorcycles. He decided not to branch out and committed himself to one venture—making two-wheelers. The business was started by his father Brijmohan Munjal and passed on to him. During his father's time the problems were different—Brijmohan took the company from a cycle components' manufacturer to a cycle maker and then entered into a joint venture with Japan's Honda to make motorcycles.

Once Hero and Honda split, Pawan was faced with an existential crisis. But he took the challenge head-on and created an R&D department from scratch, by partnering with companies abroad. Now he has taken the Hero brand to more than thirty countries and made the world his playground. He has also made the brand the largest maker of two-wheelers in the world, no mean feat.

Analjit Singh, on the other hand, has an investor's instinct, which bore fruit through his investments in Vodafone (then Hutchinson Essar). He has tried out many successful and unsuccessful businesses before finally building what is perhaps closest to his heart—a healthcare conglomerate that we know as the Max Group today. While working on his ventures he had to simultaneously handle a bitter family feud as well. He did that with tact and a little help from his friend Sunil Mittal as a mediator. But then, like he says, 'Don't look to decide your life's projects and journey in one week. The journey will be assembled over a lifetime.'

Doing liberal arts in an India that celebrates the MBA is like asking to wear a crown of thorns. And being Lincolnian at a time when people revere the Obamas and the Merkels of the world, not to mention the Modis, is a psychological battle as well. Anand Mahindra is more at ease with cinema than commerce. I first met him almost a decade ago when he invited me to watch films as part of a festival that his group was sponsoring in New York. And the first film that I saw there was *The Kite Runner*. In many ways, Anand too is a perennial kite runner. The simple things of life delight him. He would be more at home walking around Kalaghoda in Mumbai, soaking up culture, than at the Promenade in Davos, discussing the global meltdown. His is the only confederate I know in corporate India. He runs the Mahindra Group like Abraham Lincoln ran America—with an almost pious benevolence in a world that is more shark-like. The ability to thus create a group that is powered by ideas is worthy of admiration. Anand is morphing from CEO to statesman much like Lincoln. Lincoln may never be remembered as the man who was the most powerful president of the United States, but he will certainly be remembered as the man who made the United States become a country. What Anand is toiling towards is a level of statesmanship that transcends profit-making, and hence his mantras acquire an almost ethereal spiritual tonality. His beyond-business beliefs have helped many in a myriad ways.

Anand, like many of the heads in this book, is a 'professioneur'—an entrepreneur who is also a professional, and perhaps the other way round too. His group has shown exemplary zeal in areas beyond business and he, like many successful CEOs, has exhibited unimaginable audaciousness. No right-minded Indian businessperson would have touched Satyam when that IT company's owner turned rogue. But Anand did. I have a suspicion that he did it for two reasons—business and nation. Just like he endowed Harvard University with the Mahindra Humanities Center, Anand has spawned businesses laced with passion and an abiding belief in Indian capability. He has often talked about jugaad, but that is not something he has infused any of his businesses with.

Be it farm equipment or automobiles or even the light-hearted holiday homes' business, it is almost as if Anand was dabbling in them because of his personal credo of savouring life in a poet-like manner. Whenever I see him, he reminds me of William Wordsworth; a strange example, I know, but some of his actions seem to echo what must have raced through Wordsworth's head when he saw those daffodils. I have never seen Anand call the shots as a CEO who wishes to crack the whip. He has always used trust and benevolence as his weapons of mass affection, which helps when you lead a business house that is so widespread in terms of impact. The farmer who he helps with the ploughing of land through his machinery may never see Anand's tweets, but his words are certainly an inspiration to those who plod in front of computer terminals at Tech Mahindra.

When the Mahindras launched their first SUV, many were sceptical. Today, Anand has an admirer in even his former competitor Ratan Tata. But I don't know if Anand will ever be as proud of the Scorpio as he is about the Nanhi Kalis that he helps blossom—the girl child who is at the heart of every society and yet so neglected. I don't know if the Mahindras will ever become the biggest, but with Anand at the helm, they will certainly be the bravest and brightest. He has age on his side and an unflappable nature laced with a sardonic sense of humour. There is deep insight behind every wicked smile of his. Not to mention his sense of sartorial elegance and coiffured hair. Anand Mahindra, more than anyone else, recognizes the role of optics and substance in the career trajectory of great CEOs.

It is not often that one looks out of the window to admire the pristine beauty of the Taj Mahal at sunset with another male. But my first ever meeting with Prithvi Raj Singh Oberoi (Biki) happened at his tony property, The Amar Vilas in Agra, almost a decade and a half ago. Biki is the oldest CEO profiled in this book, but perhaps with the youngest eye. We were both grappling with setting up the India chapter of the World Travel and Tourism Council (WTTC) and whilst the agenda was dreary, Biki's passion was infectious. I have never seen a man who pays as much attention to detail as Biki does. Actually, make that two men—Biki Oberoi and Analjit Singh (who at one time almost became Biki's white knight). It must drive people crazy but in a country where mediocrity reigns most of the time, Biki has created islands of excellence. I remember when the Vilases first came up, many said that they were white elephants. They probably were at the time but then Biki has always been ahead of the curve. On my part, I have a fetish for attention to detail, which is why Biki's deeds have always resonated with me. The fact that to this day, and at this age, Biki works manically, is testimony to the passion and zeal he possesses for his work as a 'humble inn-keeper' (as he often describes himself). CEOs, as I have said before, often disregard realities for the big picture that only they can see. I am certain that while Biki may have found the idea of building his Vilases daunting, he was defiant as far as fiscal logic was concerned. The one quality most great CEOs possess is the ability to insulate and isolate. They insulate themselves from a sceptical world that often comes in the way of their grand plan. And they isolate themselves from the chatter of a world that perhaps doesn't know as much as they do. Through his mantras, Biki exudes the simplicity of an uncluttered mind, but one that has been honed on the twin beds of excellence and experience.

Today, the Oberoi hotels stand apart in a world that is increasingly competitive. The group has created an Indian brand with a global footprint of excellence and that is because there is one man at the helm, who swings from dictator to benefactor depending on the need of the hour. A group that draws on people must have a patriarch who will carry a team but on his terms. For far too long, many CEOs have used their people as fodder to win awards or a name for themselves. Biki, on the other hand, has always believed that his people are not just at the heart of his business but are the business. In our many conversations, Biki has shown a rare understanding of people and of the need to inspire them to become ambassadors and beacons of excellence. If there is low attrition in the Oberoi Group, it is because Biki has created a trusted family of professionals.

While on the one hand this book profiles veterans who have proved their worth and sagacity down the years as well as illustrious heirs who have taken the family legacy to new dimensions, on the other there are the likes of Kiran Mazumdar-Shaw of Biocon, Rahul Sharma of Micromax and Kunal Bahl of Snapdeal, all of them first-time business leaders who have built their companies from scratch without having any backing from their families, or a famous name. Kiran Mazumdar-Shaw created a business out of a personal tragedy, becoming India's richest female entrepreneur in the bargain. Over the years she has dedicated herself to the cause of saving lives, which seems to drive her more than the idea of making profits. The thought of creating a cancer-treating drug came to her when she lost her dear friend to the dreaded disease, an event that changed her life forever. It was further spurred when Kiran's husband John was diagnosed with cancer as well; luckily, he was fully cured. As thousands more have been, thanks to the research and innovations by Biocon.

Rahul Sharma and Kunal Bahl represent businesses of modern ideas that harness today's technology and tap into the needs and desires of the new-age consumer. Both of them started out small, but their aspirations were big. Rahul went ahead to create India's largest mobile handset company, by focusing on affordability and innovation—it now provides stiff competition to the likes of Nokia, BlackBerry and Samsung. And with his passion for fast cars and living the good life, Rahul is an inspiration for today's youth.

Kunal, on the other hand, won the trust and confidence of Ratan Tata, who is now an investor in Snapdeal, India's largest e-commerce marketplace. The pivots the company has gone through are many, but Kunal's resilience is worth noting. His mantras of scale and speed have helped him rise from standing outside merchants' offices for hours to convince them to come on board, to competing with one of the world's biggest companies, Amazon.

The book also has more incredible stories of entrepreneurs who have made it against all odds. Such as Kushal Pal Singh of DLF, who literally created Gurgaon, and brought DLF back into the business of real estate after two decades through sheer business savvy. A former army man, he rose to become India's richest real-estate baron for the longest time.

Kishore Biyani of the Future Group, often called the retail king of India, talks from his heart, and that's how he runs his business too. Starting from a single shop in Kolkata to creating multibrand retail chain Pantaloons, selling it off and then reinventing the wheel with Big Bazaar and other retail ventures, he's come full circle. A maverick in the traditional Indian industry, he redefined retailing in India by introducing large-format retail stores.

The other man in Kishore's space is Sanjiv Goenka of the RP-Sanjiv Goenka group, with his Spencer's. However, if that was the only business Sanjiv had his finger in, Kishore would have been more worried. Sanjiv, who inherited his business empire from his father, is also involved in power generation, media and carbon black. He had bought an ailing Calcutta Electric Supply Corporation (CESC) when he was just twenty-eight, that too without consulting his father. Many years later, CESC is the group's flagship.

Then there are those who have brought India and the world closer by establishing a global brand in India and helping it adjust to and imbibe the Indian ethos. Atul Singh, group president, Asia Pacific, of Coca-Cola, was specially brought in to steer the global conglomerate's India arm in its toughest times when issues of pesticides in its drinks were paramount and the courts were after the company's life. At the same time he had to wage a battle for market share with arch rival Pepsi.

Rajiv Memani of Ernst & Young (EY) more or less singlehandedly set up EY's India practice, which today is one of the 'Big Four' professional services firms in the country. A follower of Swami Vivekananda, Rajiv has adapted many of the visionary's teachings to his work, and the result is there for all to see. Almost all his clients have taken his word, even against their own instincts, when it came to big business decisions, and it has paid off.

If trust, both in the CEO and the business he heads, is an important ingredient, then Adi Godrej exemplifies this quality. Adi has continued to imbibe and transmit the highest quality of governance and transparency in all that the Godrej Group does. India is blessed to have CEOs like him.

Then there are the two airline barons, Naresh Goyal and Aditya

Ghosh. Naresh founded Jet Airways and Aditya is the star CEO who made IndiGo India's No. 1 airline. Both encountered different kinds of problems, but faced them with aplomb. Naresh, with the blessings of J.R.D. Tata, started out at a time when the airlines business had grudgingly opened up for private players. His airline, Jet Airways, was not even permitted to put up its schedule of flights, but Naresh found an innovative way around the rules to inform his customers of their flight timings. In a way, he was part of the development of the airlines industry in India, and Jet is still the second-largest carrier in the country. Aditya Ghosh is a man of focus who is obsessed with details and low costs, and is against wastage. IndiGo is one of the few profitable airlines in the country at a time when almost all the others have closed down or are in dire straits. It takes its cues from global airways like Singapore Airlines.

And last but not the least is the story of two bankers who took HDFC from housing finance to one of the biggest names in Indian banking—Deepak Parekh and his most trusted lieutenant, Aditya Puri. Both of them have made HDFC what it is today.

Truth be told, there are many great leaders who are not included in this book. But that doesn't rob them of their well-earned sheen. A book is, after all, a book and not an encyclopedia. However, this is the first time that a constellation of business leaders as bright as this has been part of a single book. The gathering of these luminaries is a tribute to the evolution of corporate India and an indication of where this country is headed. The CEOs you will meet and rediscover in here have shown grit, determination and, above all, an avowed passion in their drive to be the best at what they do. They also represent various sectors in this country, which just goes to prove that great CEOs inspire and have a positive impact on all those whose lives they touch, no matter which business they helm.

Some of them have success mantras in common but this is unsurprising because there are some underlying principles that are often the bedrock of business leadership. But the manner in which these leaders enact the principles may vary, as is reflected in this book.

I am sure that with the passage of time, many of these stories will be rewritten, as they should be. Many names will probably be added to this illustrious collection. But the ultimate test will be not just their success in making it big, but more critically, in being the best.

As I speculate on the future of this country, I cannot but help express my gratitude to these men and women for doing what they are doing and helping the nation, while, of course, looking after their own interests and those of their shareholders. This is not a book that will rest at merely chronicling achievements. The idea is to celebrate these leaders for who they are and what they represent.

This is a book that should inspire you with tales of what is possible and give you food for thought. After all, *Mantras for Success* is the first of its kind in terms of getting this stellar cast of superb business leaders to share what they believe has led to the enormous success they have achieved. You don't have to be a business leader or a management student to benefit from this book; if it can ignite passion and stoke excellence in everyone who reads it, it would have achieved what it set out to do.

—Suhel Seth

RATAN TATA

Ratan Naval Tata is currently the chairman emeritus of Tata Sons, the holding company of the Tata group. He served as the chairman of Tata Sons from 1991 till December 2012. During his tenure, the group's revenues grew manifold, totalling over $100 billion in 2011-12. He was also responsible for expanding the group's operations to more than 100 countries over six continents. The Government of India honoured Ratan Tata with its second-highest civilian award, the Padma Vibhushan, in 2008. The Rockefeller Foundation, the world's oldest foundation, honoured him in 2012 with a Lifetime Achievement Award for Innovation. In 2014, he became the first Indian to be awarded the Knight Grand Cross of the Order of the British Empire (GBE) since India became a republic in 1950.

THE CHANGE ARCHITECT

Ratan Tata overhauled and re-energized the country's oldest business empire, leaving a much larger and smoother-functioning Tata group for his successor, Cyrus Mistry.

2007: the fall of the Lehman Brothers that eventually sent the US into recession was yet to happen. But Ford Motors, the inventors of the iconic Ford Model T and the fifth-largest car company in the world, was already in trouble, failing to attract buyers in the US, its home country and also its largest buyer base. In order to save itself from bankruptcy, it had only one option—to sell its stakes in foreign car companies. Volvo was sold to Chinese carmaker Zhejianj Geely Holdings and the majority stake in Aston Martin was sold to a consortium of investors. Next in line was the Jaguar, along with the Land Rover (JLR).

Ford had bought Jaguar in 1989 and the Land Rover from BMW in 2000. In the two decades that Ford owned Jaguar, it consistently made losses. But when Jaguar finally started showing some signs of a turnaround, Ford had no money to pump into the guzzler.

Looking to buy JLR were a clutch of private equity players, as well as two Indian companies, Tata Motors and Mahindra & Mahindra. Ironically, both the Indian groups specialized in making Sports Utility Vehicles or SUVs (the Tatas, however, had also seen some success with their made-in-India hatchback, Indica, and the compact sedan, Indigo).

Though Ford was briefly interested in selling JLR to the private equity guys, the company was unsure if the brands could survive outside of a large automobile group. That left Ford with only two options, Tata and Mahindra. Eventually Mahindra backed out, and Tata Motors sealed the deal at $2.3 billion in 2008. 'Think big and be bold in your actions. Lead and never follow,' says Ratan Tata, about sealing this audacious deal.

And soon enough, the Lehman crisis engulfed Detroit auto majors like General Motors and Chrysler as well. Saab Automobile, which was then making double the number of cars that Jaguar manufactured, had to close shop. Countries went into recession, people lost jobs and companies closed down. And, of course, car sales plummeted.

Had it not been for Ratan Tata, the then seventy-year-old patriarch and custodian of the Tata group, the deal perhaps would never have happened. Ratan romanticized British cars, and insiders say that the decision to buy JLR came straight from him.

The first year after the acquisition was tough. JLR sales dropped by a third, and there was a loss of $468 million on Tata Motors' balance sheets. At one point of time, it was difficult to meet the salaries of JLR's 20,000 employees. About 2,000 people were asked to leave, and the management considered closing one factory.

Finally in 2009, Ratan was able to raise $800 million from the European Investment Bank and some private funds. And soon enough, JLR's fortunes changed. Three years after the purchase, JLR managed to make profits close to what been had spent to buy the company.

Ratan spent a huge amount of time focusing on streamlining operations and cutting costs. 'And they've been very decisive in choosing the management. But once they're in place, they leave them to get on with it, unlike Ford. They're long-term, committed, patient owners. All the things you want,' Professor David Bailey of Coventry University told the *Daily Mail* in a 2012 article.[1] Seven years later, JLR has become Tata Motors' saviour while the Indian counterpart is struggling in a falling market with old product platforms, some of them older than a decade.

JLR is not a one-off, though. In the past, Ratan has spearheaded large global deals like buying Corus (known as British Steel earlier) in 2007, and Tetley tea in 2000. Under his chairmanship, since 1991, the salt-to-software Tata group has scaled unprecedented heights. Tata Consultancy Services (TCS) has become India's largest IT company. The Tata Nano, a low-cost car aimed at being affordable to all, has hit the

---

[1] Ben Oliver, 'Made in Britain. Saved in India. Craved in China: How the Jaguar Land Rover Group was Saved...by Indian Cash and Chinese Drivers', *MailOnline*, 25 August 2012.

Indian roads. The Taj Hotels, Resorts and Palaces is a name to reckon with in the luxury hospitality space.

Cornell to Bombay House

Ratan Tata is the great-grandson of Jamsetji Nusserwanji Tata, founder of the Tata group. He went to school in Bombay, and college in Cornell University, where he studied architecture. He then found himself a job with American technology firm International Business Machines (IBM). But he had to return in 1962 because his grandfather was unwell. Soon, he found himself drawn into the family business.

His first assignment was as an apprentice on the shop floor at Tata Steel, then known as TISCO (Tata Iron and Steel Company), in Jamshedpur, in erstwhile Bihar (now in Jharkhand). The Tata group has a huge factory there and has established a township around it. The city has an overbearing presence of the Tata family, so much so that often it is simply called 'Tata', short for Tatanagar, by the locals.

Nine years later, Ratan was asked to take over the operations of Tata's National Radio and Electronics Company Ltd (Nelco) which then made radios, radiograms and some other engineering products. The company was in bad shape, running into 40 per cent losses. Under Ratan, the company's financial condition stabilized, but only for a short while.

Ratan then went off to Harvard Business School for its Advanced Management Program in 1975. When he returned in 1977, he was asked to help turn around another ailing group company,

Empress Mills. The company was not facing operational and competitive challenges as much as it was being affected by the plague of unionization—led by legendary union leader Datta Samant—which had infested deep into the textile mills of Bombay. However, for the next nine years, Ratan managed to keep the company afloat.

By then he had already proved his ability to the then chairman, J.R.D. Tata, who named Ratan as his successor in 1991, over old hands such as Darbari Seth, Ajit Baburao Kerkar and Russi Mody. According to J.R.D.'s biographer, R.M. Lala, the reason he chose Ratan as his inheritor in 1991 was: '[...] because of his memory. Ratan will be more like me.'

And, as they say, everything else is history.

The Tata that Ratan Built

Ratan took over the reins of the conglomerate when the economy was opening up. Many companies that were flourishing in those days, like the ones owned by the Thapars, the Mafatlals, the Walchands, the DCM Group and the Modis, have over the years either disintegrated or been reduced to a few thousand crore rupees of revenue. Some experts say that Ratan Tata was the best thing that could have happened to the Tata group. Since 1991, the revenue of the group has grown to ₹475,721 crore in 2011-12 (when Ratan retired) from a mere ₹50,000 crore in 2001-02. Its net profit has gone up fifty-two times, and it makes more money than Mukesh Ambani's Reliance Industries Ltd.

When Ratan took over the company from his uncle in 1991, he had to fight internal satraps in the Bombay House who were deep-rooted and, at one time, more powerful than the chairman himself. They were either made to leave or rendered less powerful. Today Bombay House, the headquarters of the Tata group, reflects what Ratan created in the past two decades.

'Then Ratan Tata had to assimilate a homogeneous loose confederation of 80-odd disparate companies with high-profile no-nonsense chairmen,' wrote Sandeep Bamzai in an article for *Mail Today*[2]. The story of RNT, as he is called inside Bombay House, and the transformation he brought about in the Tata group, resembles the changing face of India's economy towards a more open and global one, shedding dogmas and eyeing growth.

Over the years, while Ratan grew the company organically and helped its businesses burgeon (for example, TCS made ₹818,094 million in 2013-14), he also went on an aggressive acquisition spree which completely cemented the group's global plans.

It began with the acquisition of Tetley, UK's largest tea maker, for $450 million in 2000. Tetley was much bigger than Tata Tea, so the group did a leveraged buyout by taking help from banks to fund two-thirds of the acquisition cost. For about five years, Tetley continued operating as a separate company before it was integrated with Tata Tea. During this period, Tata Tea was aligned with the processes and style of Tetley. In 2005, the integration was completed. The deal was the largest

---

[2]Sandeep Bamzai, 'End of an Era: Ratan Tata to Retire Today, Cyrus Mistry to Succeed Him', *Mail Today*, 28 December 2012.

28 | Mantras for Success

Indian buyout of an international brand. It helped Ratan learn a lot about global mergers and acquisitions. 'Take decisions and actions based on what you believe is the right thing to do—even if these actions are difficult, unpopular or emotionally hard,' he says.

Eventually, he acquired many more companies—the Indian government-owned CMC Ltd in 2001; a controlling stake in Videsh Sanchar Nigam Limited (VSNL) in 2002, which was later renamed Tata Communications; the South Korean Daewoo Motors, which makes heavy vehicles, in 2004; Singapore's NatSteel in 2005; and New York-based The Pierre hotel, also in 2005.

In 2007, Ratan did it again. The demand for steel in the European market was at an all-time high. Anglo-Dutch steel maker Corus was on sale. Tata picked it up for $13 billion, and the company is now called Tata Steel Europe. The deal made Tata the world's fifth-largest steel maker.

But with the fall of the Lehman Brothers, Europe saw a steep decline in the demand for steel. The timing was wrong, but many would today say that Ratan's decision wasn't. While people doubted the Corus deal, Ratan remained committed. In order to combat the falling demand, Tata Steel is undergoing a restructuring programme.

'In the last few years, Tata Steel has undertaken several initiatives to save costs and to align supply with the falling demand. While these initiatives have resulted in thousands of job cuts, the worsening demand in Europe has far outpaced the benefits on the cost side. The latest restructuring will affect management and administrative functions at its plants in Scunthorpe, Teesside and Workington in the United Kingdom,' wrote Ishita Ayan Dutt in *Business Standard* in 2013.[3]

The same article also mentioned: '...it will build a new £15-million furnace at its Stocksbridge site in the UK, which it expects to commission in early 2015. The new furnace will enable Tata Steel Europe to address demand from the aerospace and oil and gas industries.' The company also plans to double its annual output to 125,000 tonnes from the Hayange plant in Lorraine, France, by opening a new heat-treatment plant.

In 2013, Tata Steel signed a multi-crore deal with Network Rail, which runs and owns the UK's rail infrastructure. It now sources 95 per cent of its steel from Tata Steel.

The list goes on and on. In early 2000, Ratan told some journalists that he wanted to create an affordable four-wheeler for two-wheeler users who could not afford a car. That vision was developed into the Tata Nano. When the Nano plant got into a political tangle in the village of Singur in West Bengal over land acquisition issues and production stopped, Tata moved lock, stock and barrel from Singur to Sanand in Gujarat and resumed production. 'Challenge the unchallenged. There is always scope of addressing something that seems impossible and achieving surprising results,' believes Ratan.

Recently, Ratan realized that the fully made-in-India Indica and Indigo would need to replaced, so before he retired he

---

[3]Ishita Ayan Dutt, 'Tata Steel Retools to Save its Corus Business', *Business Standard*, 7 November 2013.

ensured that at least two new Tata cars (a hatchback and a sedan) hit the Indian roads—the Bolt and the Zest. His last joint venture was with the US-based coffee chain, Starbucks, in 2012. Earlier, Tata had bought the US-based coffeemaker Eight O'Clock, and coffee alone accounts for 25 per cent of Tata's beverage revenue.

Ratan, who loves flying and is a trained pilot, recently returned to the airlines business after more than fifty years with partnerships with AirAsia and Singapore Airlines.

On 28 December 2012, Ratan retired and Cyrus Mistry took over. When Ratan became the chairman, he was fifty-four. Cyrus is forty-six and can achieve a lot more, as Ratan has already switched the group to cruise control.

Even as he overhauled the group's business and vision, Ratan never forgot the high ethical standards of the Tata group and has continued to maintain them. 'Set the ethical and value-based tone of your organization. Accept that colleagues will do what they see you doing,' he says. He also believes, 'Be fair (not just kind) to all those you deal with, irrespective of who they are.'

Now he spends a lot of time at his residence, Cabins, with his two Alsatians. He has invested in the Indian e-commerce company Snapdeal in a personal capacity. And while he continues to be chairman emeritus of the Tata group, and watches over what he has created, he will now go back to some of his hobbies—playing the piano and flying. His able guidance and towering shadow over the Tata group will only add value to Mistry's leadership.

RATAN TATA'S MANTRAS FOR SUCCESS

Take decisions and actions based on what you believe is the right thing to do—even if these actions are difficult, unpopular or emotionally hard.

Challenge the unchallenged. There is always scope of addressing something that seems impossible and achieving surprising results.

Set the ethical and value-based tone of your organization. Accept that colleagues will do what they see you doing.

Be fair (not just kind) to all those you deal with, irrespective of who they are.

Think big and be bold in your actions.
Lead and never follow.

MUKESH AMBANI

The richest person in India for eight years running, Mukesh Ambani joined Reliance Industries Ltd (RIL) in 1981. He has been the chairman and managing director since July 2002. In 2009, he was ranked the fifth best-performing CEO in the world by the *Harvard Business Review* in its ranking of the top 50 global CEOs. In 2013, he was conferred the title of Entrepreneur of the Decade by the All India Management Association. He has led Reliance and made it the second-largest company in India, both in terms of revenue and public trading. In 2013, it was ranked 99 on the *Fortune* Global 500 list of the world's biggest corporations.

THE UNSTOPPABLE MAGNATE

Mukesh Ambani spent part of his childhood in a chawl. Now he lives in a 27-storey skyscraper. Meet the man who took forward his father's vision to create India's largest business conglomerate.

Mukesh Ambani himself wouldn't perhaps have thought that he, whose childhood was spent in a chawl (typical Mumbai tenements where many families occupy small rooms), would one day become India's richest person. A business that his father, Dhirubhai Ambani, started in 1958 slowly became one of India's biggest business empires.

Recalling the company's origins, Mukesh says, 'When my father Shri Dhirubhai Ambani dreamt of setting up India's largest enterprise, many people told him it was impossible. However, their scepticism turned out to be no match for his indomitable will.' Dhirubhai started Reliance as a commodity-trading and export house and went on to become one of the country's biggest businessmen in his time. By the 1980s, Reliance had grown into a large textile company with its signature brand

Vimal, and the family no longer had to live in the chawl.

In 1986, when Mukesh Ambani was just twenty-nine, Dhirubhai suffered his first stroke, which paralysed his right hand. Suddenly Mukesh and his younger brother Anil (two years younger) had to shoulder a lot of responsibility. In the next sixteen years, both brothers became a force to reckon with. Dhirubhai was always there as the guiding light, but now Mukesh steered the company into the areas of petroleum, gas, telecom and retail.

Dhirubhai had a second stroke in 2002, which proved fatal. Thereafter, Mukesh and Anil took over the management of Reliance Industries. By then, both of them had already learnt all that was required to run a conglomerate of this size and scale—whether it was expansion, liaising with the government or starting new business verticals.

There was a split in the family in 2004, after Dhirubhai's death. Reliance was broken into two parts. Anil kept the telecom, power and investment businesses. Mukesh got Reliance Industries. While Anil named his conglomerate Anil Dhirubhai Ambani Group (ADAG), Mukesh continued with the name Reliance Industries. Mukesh and Anil now run their separate companies, which once comprised the entire Reliance group.

Today, Mukesh's Reliance Industries' market capital of $57 billion is more than the gross domestic product of countries like Croatia and Uzbekistan. And he is the country's most powerful man, who runs his businesses like no one else, and is known to take unprecedented risks. According to *Forbes*, his net worth is $22.2 billion[1]. Apart from his assets worth billions of dollars, both personal and industrial, Mukesh also owns a cricket team in the Indian Premier League—the Mumbai Indians.

The power, status and wealth the Ambanis have acquired came with a lot of hard work, and after overcoming many challenges. Mukesh likes to introspect and remember the difficult times the company, his father and the family have gone through. 'In our about five decades of existence, we have seen our share of hurdles and difficulties. Counter[ed] these by relying on meticulous planning, flawless execution and developing an ability to anticipate problems. Never give up optimism, not even when faced by stubborn and unforeseen adversities,' is his advice.

He gives an example of how Reliance steered around difficult situations: 'When Reliance decided to go ahead with building a petroleum refinery we faced much uncertainty—the administered price regime was still on, reforms were unfolding only gradually, and there were no guarantees of profits in a deregulated regime.' However, the Ambanis continued with the project, defying conventional wisdom and against expert advice, because in this adversity they saw opportunity. 'It is this positive streak combined with a sense of speed that will allow organizations to find opportunities worth exploring even in the most difficult of times.'

'Excellence' is Mukesh's catchword. 'Function with the aim of being the best at everything you do—not only in India, but across the world. Whether it is infrastructure, business processes

---

[1] *Forbes*, http://www.forbes.com/profile/mukesh-ambani/, accessed on 13 November 2014.

or people, always aim for the best of the best. In Reliance, our passion lies in mega-sized projects, the most advanced technologies and the highest levels of productivity.'

All of this would not have been possible without the people working for him, the ones he swears by. He calls them the 'Reliance Family'. Some of them are his friends since childhood, some he has built strong bonds with in the last three decades, and some are blood relations. 'I would go even further to say that our people are the lifeblood of Reliance. Build relationships with employees and partners on the foundation of trust and strengthen them through shared goals.'

Anand Jain is his classmate and is known to be Mukesh's eyes and ears. Manoj Modi is a friend from the University Department of Chemical Technology (UDCT), Mumbai, and is ofen referred to as the man who delves into the details. Nikhil and Hetal Meswani are his cousins, and have critical roles in the company.

Reliance invests heavily in technology. The company had invested ₹300 crore in technology till 2007, which Mukesh said would help in bringing transparency and accountability to the company.

Reliance was the first company to introduce video conferencing in India. In the 1980s, it bought helicopters to save time on travel. Some industry watchers thought these were just flashy moves to gain media attention, but Mukesh begs to differ. 'For us, it was facilitating investments... Let me also answer the flipside. We have not invested well in marketing ourselves. It is partly because of my trait. I believe that if my conviction is right, I will not need to go and explain myself to anyone. I believed that ultimately everyone will figure out what you are. We are changing this approach,' he said in an interview to *MoneyLIFE* in 2007.[2]

Some of the traits that have led him to such heights today were formed when he was a kid. Dhirubhai always allowed the siblings—Dipti, Nina, Anil and Mukesh—to do what they wanted to and, in Mukesh's words, they weren't 'micro-managed'. This helped him develop his own skills and become self-reliant.

In an article in *The New York Times* on 15 June 2008, a comparison was made between Mukesh Ambani and Mahatma Gandhi: 'In the last century, Mohandas K. Gandhi was India's most famous and powerful private citizen. Today, Mr. Ambani is widely regarded as playing that role, though in a very different way… Mr. Gandhi was a champion of the village, a skeptic of modernity and a man focused on spiritual purity. Mr. Ambani is a champion of the city, a burier of the past and a man who deftly wields financial power.'[3]

Mukesh himself is a bit more humble. 'The aim should be to raise existing bars to unimaginable, even audacious, levels—whether it is scale, quality or something else. Don't target just growth, target exponential growth. Think big and build your very own unique and ambitious vision.'

---

[2]Sucheta Dalal and Debashis Basu, 'Mukesh Ambani on Retail and SEZ Plans', *Rediff*, http://www.rediff.com/money/2007/jan/19inter.htm, accessed on 8 January 2015.
[3]Anand Girihardas, 'Indian to the Core, and an Oligarch', *The New York Times*, 15 June 2008.

Businesses of the Future

Back when the business split, the two brothers had decided not to compete with each other. But barely a few years later, Mukesh also announced his foray into telecom. By then the sibling rivalry was over—both Mukesh and Anil had realized that they needed each other to derive maximum benefit from India's telecom boom. In the years that followed, Mukesh's telecom venture, Reliance Jio Infocom Limited (RJIL), did many partnerships with Anil's Reliance Communications, like sharing infrastructure.

The 2010 telecom auctions of 3G and broadband wireless access spectrum had just concluded. Infotel Broadband, owned by Mahendra Nahata, had bought BWA spectrum, which allowed next generation data services in twenty-two circles. Reliance bought up 95 per cent of Infotel (the company that is now called RJIL). This telecom venture is estimated to cross $50 billion of investment, and Mukesh has made significant announcements of tie-ups with his younger brother to share telecom infrastructure and offer data services.

Mukesh had shown poise in executing mega-projects even before coming out of his father's shadow. In his words, 'What businesses do is important, but why they do it is even more telling. Measure success not only based on what returns the shareholders received, but also on how many lives were touched through products and services.'

The Jamnagar Refinery is one such example. It was built at a record-breaking speed of less than three years, commissioned in 1999. The refinery is able to process virtually every type of crude oil in the world and, in Mukesh's words, 'remains one of the most complex refineries in the world.' It has a green belt surrounding it, something he takes pride in. 'An arid desert was converted into a lush mango plantation, and today Reliance is one of India's largest exporters of mangoes,' he says.

Of the 800 million acres of land bank that India has, only 500 million is being used for some sort of agriculture. Another 150 million acres, Mukesh thinks, can be converted into productive land. In the interview to *MoneyLIFE*, he said that the food market was bigger than the software services market and that, if tapped well, the 'spin-offs' would create a huge boom in consumption.[4] Right now, he is not involved directly in any food-related business, but who knows, tomorrow he might be.

In other countries, Mukesh might have been treated as a demi-god, given his views. He talks about creating jobs, and building infrastructure like in Shenzhen and Shanghai. 'When I put out a comparative chart, I should be able to tell big employers: this is how we compare with Singapore, Dubai, Shenzhen or Malaysia and Korea. On every parameter, I should beat others in cost and quality of infrastructure [...] and talent,' he said in his interview.[5]

---

[4] Sucheta Dalal and Debashis Basu, 'Mukesh Ambani on Retail and SEZ Plans', *Rediff*, http://www.rediff.com/money/2007/jan/19inter.htm, accussed on 8 January 2015.
[5] Ibid.

India and the World

Mukesh's investments and interests are not confined solely to India. In the retail space, Reliance is tying up with Brooks Brothers and Marks and Spencer. He also sits on the boards of companies like McKinsey. He is associated with the United Nations and the global business body, the World Economic Forum. British Petroleum also invested $7.2 billion in Reliance, and also helped the company with international technology, know-how and the best business practices.

Mukesh's ventures, put together, account for 15 per cent of India's exports, 4 per cent of the country's stock market value and 3 per cent of the national tax revenue. Last year alone, it generated $8 billion of cash. The Jamnagar Refinery produces 2 per cent of the world's crude oil, reported *The Economist* (2 August 2014), making it one of the ten biggest refineries in the world.[6]

'Always remain focused on the bigger picture and do your bit to take India to the heights it seeks. Firmly believe in the Indian growth story,' is one of his mantras. Somewhere within his India Dream lie Dhirubhai's philosophies. 'Don't do business just for profits, but to touch the lives of millions of people in a positive way. Aim at fulfilling their aspirations, their needs and above all strive to make them happy. That is our bigger purpose as corporates.'

Mukesh has more reasons to believe that India is good for

---

[6]'Reimagining Ambani', *The Economist*, 2 August 2014.

Reliance. 'We are driven by the irrepressible desire that India should be next to none in the world. This has remained one of our guiding principles through the years. We believe that the fates of Reliance and India are deeply intertwined—the growth of Reliance is an integral part of the grand vision for India, and vice versa,' he says.

In many ways, this is true.

To begin with, there are huge investment outlays in petrochemicals and refineries, oil explorations and production. Once gas prices are regulated (Mukesh believes against all odds that that will happen) money will pour into Reliance's coffers. Reliance also has the largest organized retail chain network in India with close to 1,700 shops and, of course, the dream of connecting over a billion people through its telecom ventures. *The Economist* reported that analysts expect the company's profits to go up by 60 per cent in the next three years, from the $3.8 billion in March 2014.[7]

No one could sum it up better than Mukesh himself: 'We have taken money from ordinary Indians and we are their trustees.'

MUKESH AMBANI'S MANTRAS FOR SUCCESS

Never give up optimism, not even when faced by stubborn and unforeseen adversities.

---

[7] Ibid.

[A] positive streak, combined with a sense of speed, will allow organizations to find opportunities worth exploring even in the most difficult of times.

Function with the aim of being the best at everything you do—not only in India, but across the world. Whether it is infrastructure, business processes or people, always aim for the best of the best.

Build relationships with employees and partners on the foundation of trust and strengthen them through shared goals.

The aim should be to raise existing bars to unimaginable, even audacious, levels—whether it is scale, quality or something else. Don't target just growth, target exponential growth. Think big and build your very own unique and ambitious vision.

What businesses do is important, but why they do it is even more telling. Measure success not only based on what returns the shareholders received, but also on how many lives were touched through products and services.

Always remain focused on the bigger picture and do your bit to take India to the heights it seeks. Firmly believe in the Indian growth story.

Don't do business just for profits, but to touch the lives of millions of people in a positive way. Aim at fulfilling their aspirations, their needs and above all strive to make them happy.

ANAND MAHINDRA

Chairman and managing director of the $16.5 billion company, Mahindra & Mahindra Limited (M&M), Anand Mahindra was part of *Fortune* magazine's list of World's 50 Greatest Leaders in 2014. Apart from the automobiles sector, M&M is also involved in finance, insurance, IT, retail, real estate and many other fields, making it one of India's top ten industrial organizations.

Anand Mahindra was a co-promoter of Kotak Mahindra Finance Ltd, which was converted into Kotak Mahindra Bank in 2003. He is the chairman of India Design Council, the governing council of the National School of Design and Public Health Foundation of India. He is the co-founder of Naandi Danone, which delivers safe drinking water to rural areas, and the founder of the Nanhi Kali programme that provides free education to underprivileged girls.

THE GOD OF BIG THINGS

Be it the iconic Scorpio SUV or his acquisition of Satyam, Anand Mahindra has created giants within the Mahindra group and, at the same time, explored new pastures in defence and aviation.

When Narendra Modi's grey Scorpio entered the gates of the Rashtrapati Bhavan for his swearing-in ceremony on 26 May 2014, Anand Mahindra was elated. The chairman and managing director of Mahindra & Mahindra Limited (M&M) tweeted: 'On behalf of the Mahindra Group, I express enormous pride that Modiji chose our Made-in-India-with-Pride chariot to ride to Rashtrapati Bhavan.'[1]

The Scorpio might be Anand Mahindra's biggest success, but in the past twenty-six years, he has evolved the Mahindra group into a federation which, he thinks, should keep growing by leaps and bounds even when he is not around.

---

[1] "Industry Looks Forward to a New Era under Modi', *The Hindu*, 26 May 2014.

M&M wasn't always this big. Two years before Independence, it was started as a steel trading company in Bombay under the name Mahindra and Mohammed by two brothers and another collaborator. After Partition, in 1947, one of the founders, Ghulam Mohammed, moved to Pakistan as its first finance minister. The two brothers, J.C. and K.C. Mahindra, continued to run the company, which was renamed as Mahindra & Mahindra. The manufacture of the iconic Willys Jeep in India, back then, was a starting point to making their own vehicles. Today, M&M is valued at $16.5 billion; it employs over 180,000 people around the world and operates in industries such as automobiles, defence, aerospace, information technology and BPOs, financial services, hospitality and retail. And this is, in a large part, due to the strategic planning and derring-do of Anand Mahindra.

Before 1997, when Anand decided to set up a factory to indigenously develop the Scorpio, M&M was mainly known for being a rural and agricultural vehicles maker. (It still continues to reign as the world's largest tractor maker, with about 42 per cent market share in that sector.) Since he took over the company in 1989—even though his uncle, Keshub Mahindra, was still the chairman—Anand has launched a series of ventures in India with international players. One such venture was with the American car manufacturer Ford, to launch the Ford Escort in India in 1996. The car flopped, but for Anand, it was a great learning experience. The team of 300 people who developed the Escort were the ones who worked on the first-generation Scorpio.

'If you want to lead a large, complex and multi-business

organization, you have to know when and how to let go, and empower others. Empowerment is the algebraic outcome of curiosity and humility. You have to know, and believe in your gut that you are not the smartest person in the room, and that optimal strategies emerge from conversations and collaboration,' says Anand.

Had he not trusted and empowered those 300 employees and let go of the failure of the Escort, perhaps he would never have been able to create the Scorpio. Till then, only the Tata group in India had ventured into the SUV space, with their hugely successful Safari. Now it was M&M's turn, and Anand's curious mind and strong gut made Scorpio an even bigger success.

The Scorpio, over the past twelve years, has become a cult vehicle. It is the symbol of the bold and powerful—used by politicians and the police alike. Maybe Anand himself did not know that over the years this car, the manufacturing of which required an investment of ₹550 crore (the largest investment by the company at the time), would become one of India's highest-selling SUVs.

And if Anand would have ridden solely on the success of the Scorpio, he would perhaps not have got the title of 'Renaissance Man'[2]. 'Success requires, above all, a deep desire to excel, and be the best that you can be, given the cards that you were dealt when you came into the world,' says Anand.

The M&M that we see today is an outcome of these mantras.

---

[2]Thomas A. Stewart and Anand P. Raman, 'Finding a Higher Gear', *Harvard Business Review*, July 2008.

The God of Big Things

Like the Tata group, Anand does not call his company a conglomerate, he calls it a federation—the company is ring-fenced from damages and can self-finance and grow and even afford to make a few mistakes. According to him, an organization like this can grow infinitely.

In 2011, M&M bought a majority stake in Korean automobile manufacturer SsangYong Motor, which helped it leapfrog into the premium league of SUVs. The number of SsangYong vehicles sold in India is small, but the company has a significant presence in the Latin American and Southeast Asian markets. Anand also acquired Reva, the electric car company, in 2010, which is now called Mahindra Reva Electric Vehicles Pvt. Ltd.

But mistakes?

Sometimes, yes. In 1994, M&M partnered with the Spanish firm MONDRAGON Corporation to set up a castings plant because the tractor industry was facing a shortage of metallurgical castings. But then there was a sudden slump in the tractors' market, and Anand decided to exit. 'This would have been the beginning of the components sector. And we regretted it greatly when the market took off and one of our biggest supply chain constraints was quality castings. That taught me to never look at investment decisions over a short period of time,' said Anand to *Forbes*.[3]

But Anand's most audacious investment by far was buying Satyam Computer Services in 2010.

---

[3] Ashish K. Mishra, 'Anand Mahindra: The Federator', *Forbes India*, 28 October 2013.

Where the Fearless Tread

Anand was interested in Satyam even before the scam happened. The now-infamous founder of Satyam Computers, B. Ramalinga Raju, and he were on the board of the Indian School of Business. At one of the board meetings, he asked Raju if he would consider a merger with Tech Mahindra Limited (TechM), M&M's IT business. TechM was already worth $800 million, but about 90 per cent of its business was coming from serving telecom customers, thanks to British Telecom, which was also a shareholder in the company.

In 2009, Raju wrote to the regulators that he had been cooking Satyam's books. He went to jail, and Satyam was up for sale. First, Anand went to Vineet Nayar, TechM's CEO, to ask if he could turn the company around and bring it out of its tainted past. Then he called up some of Satyam's customers, who were happy with the services. And, to take into account all factors, he called up Microsoft's B. Kevin Turner and SAP's Bill McDermott to gauge the level of competence of the people working at Satyam. Once he had their feedback, he told Vineet and his team to start designing a plan to rebuild Satyam. All this happened even before Anand had run his decision to buy Satyam by the company board. But he was confident that the board would come around, which they did, eventually. The company was renamed Mahindra Satyam.

In the years to come, not only did Satyam make a spectacular turnaround, but the acquisition and merger made TechM the country's fifth-largest IT company—after TCS, Infosys, Wipro and HCL Technologies (Cognizant Technologies, which is bigger than TechM, is listed abroad). At the time of the merger, nearly all of TechM's clients were from telecom businesses around the world, which made the business risky, but the Satyam merger added a variety of new clients from other sectors. This gave TechM the right business mix, since over-dependence on one sector is not financially prudent, especially in times of a downturn.

This is where Anand's success mantra finds its best place. 'In an increasingly complex and confusing world, I find that I can rely on my internal "GPS" system for directions in large measure because of my liberal arts education. What that provided me was the capacity to leverage right-brain thinking and see the forest beyond the trees. Larger patterns and opportunities emerge, even when seemingly confronted by a maze of overgrown hedges in the immediate foreground.'

M&M would not have succeeded to the extent it has without Anand's key people. Vineet Nayar was responsible for integrating and turning around Satyam and TechM, and C.P. Gurnani, TechM's managing director, was the man behind the implementation. Pawan Goenka, former research and development executive of General Motors, was brought in for the Scorpio project, for his expertise in making engines. The Scorpio experience later helped in creating the Xylo and the XUV 500, which used the same platform as the Scorpio. Chetan Maini, another important team member, heads Reva, M&M's electric car business.

'The most important step I have ever taken is to step back and let the right individuals lead and "own" their specific sectors of business. One demonstrable success in this empowered structure leads to its cloning and, with any luck, leadership within your group can grow like a benevolent virus,' says Anand.

Beginning to 'Rise'

At the turn of the century, M&M earned $1.35 billion in revenue. A decade later, it had grown more than twelve times. While it was still much smaller than Volkswagen, General Motors and Nissan, it was more diversified. Now it was time to put a finger on the customers' pulse.

According to Anand, 'You need enormous and almost overwhelming curiosity. About everything—people, places and how things work. Curiosity is the principal enabler of learning. Even if you're not as gifted or intelligent as you'd like to be, you can outstrip those ostensibly smarter than you simply by letting your mind be a sponge for information and knowledge.'

Anand had seen the denim giant, Levi's, as well as other big brands, doing something called 'movement marketing'. The idea was to get people to interact with the company.

'In a highly competitive environment, a huge helping of humility is essential for staying ahead of the game. Humility enhances curiosity, and thus accelerates learning. Without humility, you can never be a good listener and understand the voices around you—of customers, colleagues and investors,' believes Anand.

M&M had by now become a global company with employees of diverse nationalities—Korean, Chinese, German, American and, of course, Indian. Anand thought it was time to re-emphasize the core purpose of the company, which was: 'Indians are second to none'. He talked about this in an interview with *Business Today*.[4]

Coincidentally, around this time, an M&M distributor in the US engaged an advertising firm, Strawberry Frog, founded by Scott Goodson, to know more about the company. Initially Anand did not pay much heed to this, but later he took the findings seriously.

'What he [Scott] said was that consumers are looking for companies they can trust; companies whose integrity and ideals they can believe in; companies in which they are willing to become co-stakeholders even though they were merely consumers,' Anand told *Business Today*.[5]

This finding helped in conceptualizing the 'Rise' campaign. It was about how people would, in the next few years, shape or change M&M's destiny. Extensive studies were done with existing customers as well as potential customers across several continents to understand their needs.

But Anand also had to transform the company so that 'Rise' would not merely be an advertising campaign, but something which would really change M&M at its heart. It took him a year to build a company that would be worthy of the 'Rise' campaign. After that, it was time to listen to the customers

---

[4]Kushan Mitra, 'We Will Create a System that is Impregnable', *Business Today*, 13 September 2011.
[5]Ibid.

themselves, and there was nothing better than the Internet, especially social media, for this. A digital campaign called 'Spark the Rise' was unleashed on social media. Through this, M&M developed a series of programmes to assist upcoming innovators achieve their goals. This was the way Anand thought he could enable people to 'Rise' and interact with his brand.

'Without humility, you cannot sharpen your empathy, and understand what your stakeholders are feeling and what they desire. And if you are devoid of empathy, people will not want to follow you,' he says.

And this is just the beginning. Anand has gone into several other ventures, from a relatively small one in retail with Mom & Me to a bigger stake in defence by partnering with international defence firm BAE Systems—defence being another area of interest for Anand. The company is also expected to make a ₹150 crore investment in an aviation plant near Bangalore.

At just fifty-nine, Anand Mahindra's roster of achievements is unparalleled. Considering that his uncle Keshub stepped down from the position of chairman at the age of eighty-eight, Anand certainly has a long way to go.

Anand wants to build a brand which is consumer-oriented, and that is the best legacy he can bestow on the next generation. In his words: 'The legacy I want to leave behind is for people to say, "I discovered the best in myself when I was a part of Mahindra".'

ANAND MAHINDRA'S MANTRAS FOR SUCCESS

If you want to lead a large, complex and multi-business organization, you have to know when and how to let go, and empower others. Empowerment is the algebraic outcome of curiosity and humility.

Success requires, above all, a deep desire to excel, and be the best that you can be, given the cards that you were dealt when you came into the world.

Leverage [your] right-brain thinking and see the forest beyond the trees. [This way] Larger patterns and opportunities emerge.

Step back and let the right individuals lead and 'own' their specific sectors of business. [...] with any luck, leadership within your group can grow like a benevolent virus.

You need enormous and almost overwhelming curiosity. About everything—people, places and how things work. Curiosity is the principal enabler of learning. Even if you're not as gifted or intelligent as you'd like to be, you can outstrip those ostensibly smarter than you simply by letting your mind be a sponge for information and knowledge.

In a highly competitive environment, a huge helping of humility is essential for staying ahead of the game. Humility enhances curiosity, and thus

accelerates learning. Without humility, you can never be a good listener and understand the voices around you—of customers, colleagues and investors.
And if you are devoid of empathy, people will not want to follow you.

The legacy I want to leave behind is for people to say, 'I discovered the best in myself when I was a part of Mahindra'.

KUMAR MANGALAM BIRLA

Kumar Mangalam Birla is the chairman of the Aditya Birla Group, a $40 billion-multinational company that operates in thirty-six countries across six continents in industries such as aluminium, copper, cement, textiles, telecommunications and many more. He is also the chairman of Idea Cellular Ltd, India's third largest mobile operator, and Novelis Inc., the world's premier producer of rolled aluminum products. He was given *The Economic Times*' Business Leader of the Year Award for the second time in 2013. His previous win was in 2003.

THE TAKEOVER TITAN

Living up to the Birla surname comes naturally to Kumar Mangalam Birla. What stands out, though, is how he transitioned from being an Indian entrepreneur to someone who has reached out to the world.

Kumar Mangalam Birla sums up his success mantras in four simple lines:

'Your attitude determines your altitude.'

'People are your biggest asset. Set them up to succeed. Trust and empower—demonstrate genuine respect and concern for them.'

'There are no shortcuts.'

'There is no substitute to smart, hard work.'

None of these seem difficult in theory, but in practice, killing a tiger with your bare hands might seem easier, especially when you lose your father at the young age of twenty-eight, and are suddenly thrown into heading a $2 billion business empire. At the same time, you have to live up to your renowned family name. The twenty-eight-year-old who did all this, and more, was none other than Kumar Mangalam Birla.

Takeover Tales

Over the years, Kumar Mangalam has spread the group's business to forty-two countries, with about half of the company's money coming in from international operations. (In 1995, when Kumar Mangalam took over after the death of his father, Aditya Vikram Birla, the group only had a few businesses in Egypt and its surrounding countries). Almost twenty years since he took over, the Aditya Birla Group is a $40 billion conglomerate and a leader in viscose staple fibre, palm oil, integrated aluminium, insulators, carbon black, copper and cement; India's third largest telecom company; with businesses in financial services, retail, trading, natural resources and agriculture.

Unlike most other businessmen, Kumar Mangalam believes in what is called the Parta system, which essentially means that at the end of the day, there should be cash flow coming in—a very traditional Marwari way of doing business.

As Kumar Mangalam charted his global expansion plans, acquisition was on the top of his mind. One of the companies he wanted to acquire, American aluminium maker Novelis Inc., was four times the size of Hindalco (Hindustan Aluminium Company), the Birla Group's aluminium manufacturing unit. At the time, Novelis was going through a very difficult phase. In a luncheon meeting in 2006 with then Novelis CEO Brian W.

Sturgell, Hindalco's managing director Debnarayan Bhattacharya and group CFO Sumant Sinha proposed a takeover.

A few months passed but nothing worked. But still Kumar Mangalam held on to the Novelis deal. 'It was an intimidating proposition. But after a lot of thinking, I found it too compelling an opportunity to let go of,' he said to *The Economic Times*.[1]

After the acquisition, which finally happened in 2007, Novelis had to be put back on track. One of the biggest problems was that before it was acquired by the Birla Group, it had signed multiple contracts to deliver aluminium products, but had bought the raw material at a much higher price. The cost ripped the profit margins. Finally, the company was turned around by merging the high-cost business of Novelis with the low-cost business of Hindalco and taking out redundancies. Analysts who followed the turnaround closely attributed it to continuous performance improvement. The acquisition made the Birla Group the largest producer of aluminium of the world.

But this was not the first major acquisition Kumar Mangalam had made. In 1998, he had acquired Dharani Cement Ltd and Shree Digvijay Cement Co. Ltd, in a move to consolidate the company's leadership in the cement business. In 2004, Grasim, the Birla Group's flagship cement company, acquired Larsen & Toubro's (L&T) cement division for ₹2,200 crore, which was renamed UltraTech Cement Limited. At the time, this was ranked amongst one of the largest business deals in India. It

---

[1] Kausik Datta and M. Anand, 'Inside the Novelis Turnaround', *The Economic Times*, 4 October 2010.

also made Grasim India's largest cement producer, and doubled its capacity. And, more recently in 2014, UltraTech completed the acquisition of Jaypee Cement for $600 million, making Kumar Mangalam the undisputed cement king of India.

The Birla Group became the leader in producing carbon black (a form of carbon used in tyres and other rubber products) with the help of US-based Columbian Chemicals. The deal was for $875 million—it doubled the company's capacity to 2 million tonnes and got it a foothold in European and North and South American markets.

Chickening Out

Sometimes complications arose in international deals for unanticipated reasons. Such as when chicken came in the way!

The Birlas are Marwaris—a successful business community originally hailing from the state of Rajasthan, who are vegetarians and teetotallers. None of their office campuses serve or prepare non-vegetarian food. But how could the no non-veg practice continue when 60 per cent of the company's revenue came from international operations, spread across thirty-six countries and five continents, employing 136,000 people?

Since Kumar Mangalam took over as the chairman, he has acquired $8 billion worth of business overseas, according to various news reports. 'For the moment our top management remains all-Indian, even if not all-Marwari. But I would guess that within a decade, half of our senior-most staff will be non-

Indian,' writes Kumar Mangalam in 'Butter Chicken at Birla'.[2]

In 2003, Kumar Mangalam bought a small copper mine in Australia for $12.5 million. The employees were worried about the new culture that would be brought in with the change in ownership—no alcohol and no meat.

But then finally, he saw what he had least thought of. 'And as I was reminded [of] the first time I saw butter chicken being served in a Birla canteen [...] the most difficult challenges turn out to be the ones you least expect,' he writes in *Reimagining India*.[3] But then that's part and parcel of being a global company.

And as the empire expanded, a few other things also changed. At one point of time, Kumar Mangalam would be impressed by anyone who spoke the Queen's English, but as he went to Brazil and Egypt, he came across a lot of people who were not particularly proficient in English, but extraordinary at their work. So when he came back to India, he started respecting his chartered accountants more—who often came from the smaller towns of Rajasthan, and did not speak English fluently.

Playing on Trust

Kumar Mangalam expanded fast and furious outside the country, but in India he was equally aggressive. In 2001, he launched

---

[2]Kumar Mangalam Birla, 'Butter Chicken at Birla', *Reimagining India: Unlocking the Potential of Asia's Next Superpower,* Simon & Schuster, 2013.
[3]Ibid.

Idea Cellular Ltd, which was started as a joint venture between Birla and AT&T Communication. Tata Cellular joined in later. The trio got the acronym BATATA. But soon, the Tatas exited the business and so did AT&T, in 2006. Kumar Mangalam decided to carry on with Idea Cellular. But a few years later, Idea, which started off as a brand mainly focused on the youth and was considered the least expensive as compared to Airtel and Reliance, started to fizzle out.

Kumar Mangalam decided to make his company a pan-India player. He bought telecom licences. The telecom firm also started to focus on central India, instead of the metros, unlike most of its competition. Meanwhile, there were rumours that the Birla Group would sell Idea because of the growing problems in the telecom business, such as the rise of regulatory uncertainties, cancellation of licences and price war.

But Kumar Mangalam had no such plans. Instead, he wanted Idea to be one of India's top three telecom companies. When Himanshu Kapania became the managing director of Idea in 2011, the mobile telecom industry was already changing courses—social networking sites like Facebook were becoming popular and India was slowly but surely embracing the smartphone revolution. Selling voice minutes was definitely the mass business, but the future was all about Internet data. And Idea had just won third-generation (3G) spectrum in nine out of twenty-two telecom circles in the spectrum allocation auction by the government in 2010.

For Himanshu, and for Kumar Mangalam, the biggest challenge was to see that the Idea 3G network and services' rollout happened properly. Once that was done, it was all about creating customer stickiness, so that more and more people rode the Idea network and, in turn, used more data. In the next phase, the emphasis was on offering services, whether it was Facebook or instant messaging services like Whatsapp at cheap rates, entertainment services in sachet packets and, later, bundling 3G services with affordable smartphones. After a long lull in the telecom business, when the industry started reviving in 2012, Idea became the biggest gainer. And soon, the rumours of Kumar Mangalam selling Idea died. Today, Idea has reached a market cap of over ₹60,000 crore[4], and is highly profitable. It also has the lowest debt equity ratio compared to its peers, Airtel and Reliance Communications.

In 2005, three of the Aditya Birla Group companies—Indian Rayon, Indo Gulf Fertilisers and Birla Global Finance—were merged to form Aditya Birla Nuvo. These businesses of insulators and fertilizers were cash-generating, and the cash would be used to fund new businesses that Kumar Mangalam had started—in telecom through Idea, financial services, and clothing through various brands under the flagship Madura Garments, like Peter England, Van Heusen and Louis Phillippe. But in 2009, Nuvo faced serious problems because of the global downturn and went into losses. Birla asked Rajesh Jain, joint managing director of Nuvo, to get the company back on track. So Rajesh decided to build synergies. He bargained retail space rentals for the telecom, retail and financial businesses collectively (previously, there were separate teams for each business doing

---

[4]At the time of writing.

the job). He thus got economies of scale, which helped him to get better prices.

Kumar Mangalam relies on his colleagues, be it Himanshu Kapania, or Rajesh Jain to do the cost restructuring for Nuvo and bring in synergies, or Debnarayan Bhattacharya to head the Novelis deal. He continues to be an unconventional boss. He was once seen at the funeral of one of his long-time senior employees and was, in fact, the last to leave. He is also known to visit hospitals when his employees are seriously unwell.

Kumar Mangalam wants his businesses to be as self-sufficient as possible. For example, power is one of the biggest costs involved in producing aluminium. Coal is required to generate power, so he wants Hindalco to have its own source of coal. He aims to mine bauxite and wants to set up aluminia operation. This would save some of the logistical costs, and the money saved can be ploughed back into the business. 'Once the capex (investments in plants and mines) is up and running, we can have the lowest-cost production process,' Debnarayan Bhattacharya told *Business Today* in October 2011.[5] Essentially, it means that if you are the last man standing and are adding value to your customers, you will continue to grow.

Donning the Right Attire

Even while looking at building these businesses, Kumar Mangalam didn't lose sight of the Indian consumer market. India was getting more and more globalized and branded garments were becoming

---

[5]Suman Layak, 'The Kumar System', *Business Today*, 16 October 2011.

the rage. Madura Garments had to corner the market. And it did, especially in menswear. While brands like Louis Phillippe and Van Heusen catered to the premium buyer, Peter England was the more affordable category. But Kumar Mangalam created a new shopping experience for the middle class by building exclusive Peter England stores, just like the premium brands.

In food and grocery, Aditya Birla Retail's retail chain, More, might currently not be very profitable, but it is a serious contender in the segment, along with Kishore Biyani's Big Bazaar. More is the amongst the top three retail chains in the country, and expanding fast. In 2013, the company announced plans to open sixty new supermarkets and ten new hypermarkets (a combination of supermarket and department store). This would drain the profits for a while, but Kumar Mangalam is looking at a steady growth rather than quick profits.

'So we are growing. I think it is a tough business. So you have to keep learning each day and make sure that you do not make the same mistakes and make sure that you sort of absorb that learning very quickly. So when you are talking about a business where you are working on a one per cent–two per cent margin, every single [rupee] counts. So I think we are on a very steep learning curve. I don't think there's any rush to become the largest in the retail sector because I think there is space for a lot of people here. I think the important thing is to grow steadily and have high quality of earnings,' he told *Business Today* in an interview[6].

---

[6]Chaitanya Kalbag, Suman Layak and Suveen Sinha, 'No Tearing Hurry to Expand Foreign Operations: Kumar Mangalam Birla', *Business Today*, 5 October 2011.

KUMAR MANGALAM BIRLA'S MANTRAS FOR SUCCESS

Your attitude determines your altitude.

People are your biggest asset. Set them up to succeed. Trust and empower—demonstrate genuine respect and concern for them.

There are no shortcuts.

There is no substitute to smart, hard work.

The most difficult challenges turn out to be the ones you least expect.

[Y]ou have to keep learning each day and make sure that you do not make the same mistakes and make sure that you sort of absorb that learning very quickly [...] I think the important thing is to grow steadily and have high quality of earnings.

ADI GODREJ

Adi Burjorji Godrej is the chairman of the Godrej Group, one of India's leading multinational conglomerates valued at $1.875 billion. He was the president of the Confederation of Indian Industry (CII) as well, and has led key organizations of trade and commerce. He is also the chairman of the board of the Indian School of Business. He has been a former chairman of the governing council of the Narsee Monjee Institute of Management Studies. He was awarded the Padma Bhushan in 2012.

THE CHANGEOVER MAN

Adi Godrej led the Godrej Group through a series of acquisitions, entered new businesses and expanded existing ones to create one of the foremost business empires of modern India.

Before the economic crisis of 2008, the Godrej Group was pretty comfortable with the way its businesses were running. It was a company that targeted older consumers—mothers and grandmothers. Adi Godrej, the then sixty-six-year-old patriarch of the Godrej group, did not want to change much as long as things were going smoothly.

Adi is a second-generation entrepreneur who has had a good life and, unlike many other families where siblings squabbled over the business empire, Adi and his brothers didn't. The Godrej empire dates its beginnings to the nineteenth century. Even before the economic crisis had hit the world, Adi was already one of India's richest people. He owned yachts, had visited more than seventy-five countries (Brazil being his favourite), and his wife Parmeshwar was (and still is) a famous A-list socialite.

But the global crisis engulfed everyone and Adi was no exception. When it hit, he was already trying to break out of the mould of being a 'soaps and locks maker' by venturing into real estate. The group had built premium properties like the high-rise Planet Godrej in Mumbai, but the recession slackened the demand of these apartments. Adi quickly tried to make a transition from premium properties to affordable housing. Soon, the company was building houses priced between ₹5 lakh and ₹25 lakh in Kolkata and Ahmedabad, becoming one of the first developers to start affordable housing. 'This means our sales growth will be dramatic... We will not be selling flats in ten or twenty, but in numbers of 2,000 and 5,000. So we expect rapid growth,' Adi told *Forbes* in 2009.[1]

Adi also decided to give his consumer products' business a twist—by going rural. He felt that the government would spend a huge amount of money to boost consumption in Indian villages. Till then, Godrej sold most of its products in cities and towns, while the rural market was ruled by competitors like Hindustan Unilever and Procter & Gamble (P&G). So Godrej began to give free samples of its hair dyes to barbers and introduced Godrej No. 1 soaps at ₹5 a piece. It started airing its ads on Doordarshan and All India Radio, which are the most popular in rural areas. It also added 5,000 villages in its distribution network. 'We put tremendous emphasis on continuous improvement in good times as well as bad,' says Adi. The consumer products' business was barely affected by the global slowdown as compared to the real-estate business.

---

[1]Saumya Roy, 'How Adi Godrej Got 24-Hour Confidence', *Forbes India*, 2 December 2009.

Godrej's oleochemicals business was facing problems too, and its initial public offer (IPO), planned for a while, had to be deferred.

'All the focus on rural and the segment that he concentrates [sic] come from the "customer centric culture" of GCPL [Godrej Consumer Products]... That also determines the acquisition strategy as he is rapidly building inorganic growth both within [and] outside the country,' Bala Balachandran, one of the longest-serving members of the Godrej consumer board and a professor at Northwestern University's Kellogg School of Management, told *Forbes*[2]. The group now has operations in eleven countries and gets 47 per cent of its revenue from overseas.

Adi understands business perhaps like no one else in his family. In 1963, he was fresh out of college when he joined the group that was started by his uncle Ardeshir Godrej. After three decades of his joining the group, Adi led a series of acquisitions and joint ventures that changed the image of the group forever, and turned it into one of the most dynamic companies of modern India. This proved to be a blessing, because while Godrej was changing its game, many yesteryear biggies were running out of steam.

Unlocking Potential

Ardeshir Burjorji Godrej, Adi's grand-uncle, was an unsuccessful lawyer in Zanzibar, Africa, so he decided to come back to

---

[2] Ibid.

India in 1894. He joined a pharmacy in Bombay as an assistant. After a year, he decided that he would start manufacturing surgical equipment with the made-in-India stamp. But before the business was born, he read a newspaper article on the rising crime rate in the city. He dropped the idea of making surgical equipment and decided to start manufacturing locks and safes instead. He found a place in Central Bombay, a 20 square feet room in Parel. The company was named Godrej Brothers, after Ardeshir and his brother Pirojsha (Adi's grandfather). The Godrej logo, incidentally, is Pirojsha's signature.

By 1910, Ardeshir had partnered with Boyce, his father's friend Merwanji Muncherji Cama's nephew, and the company was renamed Godrej & Boyce. Ardeshir had taken a loan from Cama in 1895 to start his business. The partnership with Boyce was short-lived, although they continued with the name Godrej & Boyce. The company made locks, safes, refrigerators and steel cupboards. In 1918, the brothers started Godrej Soaps, which were made from vegetable fat while all others were made of animal fat. They sold their soap on the tropes of ahimsa (non-violence) and being swadeshi (Indian). The product, called Chavi, was revolutionary. Today, Godrej's soaps—Godrej No. 1 and Cinthol—are still bestsellers. 'A strong emphasis on innovation, not just in products, but also in business processes, is very important,' says Adi.

Pirojsha realized that it was important for the group to diversify. India was a closed economy. Any company with more than ₹20 crore in revenue was termed a monopoly, and licences were required to do anything beyond that. It was difficult to get the requisite licences to expand, but approvals for new businesses were easier. Keeping this in mind, Pirojsha bought huge plots of land in Vikhroli, Maharashtra, in the 1940s, where he later built factories in the 1950s. The main headquarters also came up here and Adi still has his office there. As per the Monopolies and Restrictive Trade Practices Act, 1969, business expansion could only happen in backward districts, so Pirojsha ensured that the real estate in Vikhroli was utilized well.

When Adi joined the business in 1963, he was the first MBA graduate in the company. He was only twenty-one, and had completed his graduation and taken a management degree from Massachusetts Institute of Technology, USA. Godrej & Boyce at the time had a revenue of ₹8 crore and the soap business, which made ₹2 crore, was running into losses. Adi's main job was to introduce management practices and bring in cost accounting, apart from turning around the soap business. Within a year of his joining the company, he made the soap business profitable. Adi had tasted sweet success, but his journey was yet to begin.

Over the years the group has diversified into many new areas. 'All our diversifications have been logical... Our first product was locks, from where we moved to security equipment [safes], then to steel cupboards and then refrigerators. Then came typewriters—manual, electric and then electronic—and machine tools. Now we make plant[s] and equipment for oil refineries, and even work with the Indian space and nuclear programmes,' said Adi to *Forbes*.[3]

---

[3]Ibid.

The Changeover Man

Going for the Kill

In 1994, Adi stumbled upon an opportunity that would lead to something iconic. Godrej acquired Transelektra, a mosquito-repellent brand, which was also one of the first buyouts by an Indian fast-moving consumer goods (FMCG) company.

At the time, Arumugham Mahendran, who headed Transelektra, was looking for a buyer for the repellent business. He asked his friend Uday Kotak to help him find a buyer. Kotak, in turn, asked Adi if he was interested. Adi visited the Transelektra factory in Pondicherry, where Arumugham took him around. But Adi was restless and suddenly wandered off. When Arumugham finally found him, he got to know that Adi had asked a worker to show him the company books. The reason for his doing so was that Arumugham had said that the business was worth ₹60 crore annually and Adi wanted to check if that was really the case, by checking the dispatches. Once he was satisfied that it was really so, the deal was closed in a week. Adi wasn't impulsive, though. In an article in *Outlook Business*, Arumugham said, 'He laid down two conditions before signing the deal—that I should become managing director and stay on with the company for at least one year and that I should buy 5 per cent of the stock.'[4] Arumugham stayed in the company for many more years after the deal, finally leaving the firm in 2013. 'Even back in 1994, he [Adi Godrej] recognized the importance of having [one's] skin in the game and ensured it was there before he bought

---

[4]Meenakshi Radhakrishnan-Swami, 'The Godrej Guardian', *Outlook Business*, 6 July 2013.

Transelektra,' he said.[5]

Today, Transelektra's brands, Good Knight and Hit, are household names.

Around that time, India had just been liberalized and multinational giants like P&G and General Electric (GE) were looking for partners to do business in rural areas. Out of these joint ventures came marketing and product innovations like sachets of shampoos and hair dyes. Godrej partnered with P&G for a while, but the partnership did not last. Godrej never reached the same league as the Tatas or the Ambanis, because it did not grow as fast, which Adi says was intentional. 'The main financial metric for our companies are economic value added [EVA], which is profit after tax minus cost of capital (both debt and equity). A large part of our workforce is on considerable variable remuneration based on EVA improvements in their companies,' says Adi.

After 1994, Godrej did a series of acquisitions—insecticides Banish and Jet in 1995 from Sara Lee; Hexit from Hoechst Schering AgrEvo Limited in 1998; Key, Trilo and Ezee (all from Cussons) in 1999; an animal feeds' business from HLL in 2001; Keyline Brands in UK in 2005; Chittur-based Nutrine in 2006; Rapidol (Pty) Limited and Kinky, both South African brands, in 2006 and 2008 respectively; Megasari in Indonesia, Tura in Nigeria, Issue and Argencos in Argentina, Naturesse Consumer Products and Essence Consumer Products in India in 2010; Darling, an African haircare company, in three stages

---

[5]Ibid.

since 2011; Cosmética Nacional in Chile in 2012; and Colgate-Palmolive's Soft and Gentle in the UK, in 2013.

What the Future Holds

The Godrej Group has a 116-year legacy—Adi Godrej himself is seventy-two, but he has no plans to step down. He still has big plans for the group. Godrej is one of the few organizations which has a buyer base of 500 million, something few companies in India can boast of. Adi Godrej wants to take that number to a billion. The company, which had a revenue of ₹10 crore when Adi joined, registered a profit of ₹119.60 crore for the financial year of 2013-14[6]. As Adi says, 'Remember: sales is vanity, profit is sanity and cash is reality.'

In 2011, Adi announced that the group will grow ten times in ten years, which means that he is looking at a ₹1.5 trillion company by 2021. For this, the company needs to grow at a rate of 26 per cent compound annually. Till 2011, it grew at 17 per cent, and in the past three years it has grown at about 28 to 29 per cent.

One thing that might help achieve the desired rate of growth is Adi's real-estate business, which is headed by his son, also named Pirojsha. The Godrej family owns 3,500 acres of land in suburban Mumbai, which was bought by Adi's grandfather Pirojsha. That makes the Godrejs Mumbai's biggest landlords. These properties are not owned by Godrej Properties, Godrej's

---

[6]Source: http://www.godrej.com/godrej/GodrejIndustries/download/GIL_AR_Financials_Statement.pdf, accessed on 3 November 2014.

primary real-estate business, but are developed in partnership with Godrej & Boyce, a subsidiary of the Godrej Group. Godrej now also deals in home furniture.

While growing the business all there years, Adi has never neglected his health. He has said earlier that eventually he will have to leave the business but that won't happen any time soon. For years, while his children went to school, he would have breakfast with them, and after that, since he did not have anything to do at home, he would reach his office at 8 a.m.—a routine which he still follows. At the age of sixty, he trekked 42 kilometres to Mount Kailash in Tibet in a day. He walks, does isometric exercises and is punctual. 'I have always put a lot of emphasis on punctuality, planning my schedule and remaining healthy through regular exercise and maintaining a balanced diet,' he says.

Adi Godrej seems to be one of those people who never grows old in their organizations. 2021 is not far away, and Adi will surely be around to see the size of his business double.

ADI GODREJ'S MANTRAS FOR SUCCESS

We put tremendous emphasis on continuous improvement in good times as well as bad.

A strong emphasis on innovation, not just in products, but also in business processes, is very important.

Remember: sales is vanity, profit is sanity and cash is reality.

I have always put a lot of emphasis on punctuality, planning my schedule and remaining healthy through regular exercise and maintaining a balanced diet.

SUNIL BHARTI MITTAL

Sunil Bharti Mittal is the executive chairman and group chief executive officer of Bharti Enterprises Limited, a company which he founded in 1976. Today, Bharti Enterprises operates in sectors such as telecommunications, financial services, retail, realty and agri products. Bharti Airtel, part of the group, is India's largest telecom operator and the fourth-largest telecom company in the world, according to subscriber base, and has operations in twenty countries across Asia and Africa. Sunil Mittal was awarded the Padma Bhushan in 2007.

A PHONE-MAN'S LEGACY

How a man who once made crankshafts for bicycles created a company valued at more than a trillion rupees.

Sunil Bharti Mittal had a three-hour-long meeting in Paris with the head of France's second-largest telecom company, Vivendi, in 1992. This was before anybody in India had even experienced what a mobile phone could do. He wanted Vivendi to partner with him to start cellular services in Delhi under the brand name Airtel.

Sunil knew it would be a 'once-in-a-lifetime bet'.

He felt he had a very good meeting with the Vivendi head and came back to Delhi satisfied. However, he soon realized that Vivendi was keen to partner with B.K. Modi's Spice Communications. B.K. Modi was a powerful business name from the pre-liberalization era, while Sunil Mittal had just risen from being a crankshaft-maker to phone-maker.

But Sunil wasn't ready to give up so easily. He asked the Vivendi head to hear him out one last time. To his amazement, the man listened and decided to go with Sunil after all. Vivendi never repented the decision. Sunil did everything he could to create the enterprise. He borrowed, took huge loans and made deferred payments. He took his first licences in Delhi and three other metros.

Today Bharti Enterprises, which bears Sunil's middle name, has grown beyond telecom, venturing into areas of real estate, insurance and retail. Bharti Airtel is the jewel in Sunil's crown—the telecom company is the largest in India and even has operations in Africa. It is valued at ₹1.41 trillion[1]. Meanwhile, many telecom entrepreneurs of Sunil's time are no longer in business—B.K. Modi, Shashi and Ravi Ruia of Hutchison Essar, Rajeev Chandrasekhar (Sunil's friend) who started BPL Mobile and Vinay Rai of Koshika Telecom.

Sunil is still going strong.

He is, in essence, a dreamer, and that's his first success mantra. He says emphatically, 'No dream is too big,' and further explains: 'Two decades back, a company with a turnover of ₹25 crore aspiring to enter mobile telephony was scoffed at. Today, the company is the fourth-largest mobile operator in the world.'

But being a dreamer would not have been enough to scale such heights without foresight, knowing how to manage people and having the ability to take risks.

---

[1] At the time of writing.

Before Memory Fades

People remember Airtel as it has become in the last one-and-a-half decade, but fifty-seven-year-old Sunil reveals that the company has a long history. He starts with how his company got its name. Sunil's father, Sat Paul Mittal, was a parliamentarian. He gave his son the middle name Bharti, which essentially means India, the motherland; and he also gave Sunil the seed capital to start his venture.

In 1976, when Sunil was just eighteen, he took a loan of ₹20,000 (a huge amount then) from his father. Initially he made bicycle parts, then shifted gears to import power generators from Suzuki Motor Company in Japan. Soon the business started doing well, but those were the days of the licence raj, where the government would give licences to import, manufacture or trade.

In 1984, Sunil lost almost everything he had built when the government banned the import of generators. 'So overnight there was no business,' said Sunil to *Financial Times*. 'These were the times when entrepreneurs were at the mercy of government policy and you always had to be prepared, sitting in your hot seat, to take a jump and plunge into something else as soon as the government hit you with a change in policy.'[2]

After that, there was nothing much to do for him. He decided to go on a short trip to Taiwan. When he was there, he landed up at the trade fair one day, where he saw a push-button phone. He decided to bring them to India. Initially, he sourced the

---

[2] Jo Johnson, 'Profile: Sunil Bharti Mittal', *Financial Times*, 27 November 2006.

phones from Taiwan, but soon got a licence to set up a factory in Ludhiana to manufacture them. For this venture he partnered with Siemens. The first push-button phones were sold under the brand name 'Mitbrau', an abbreviated name for Mittal Brothers (his other two brothers are Rakesh and Rajan Mittal).

Then, in 1991, India's economy was in the dumps—gross domestic product growth had fallen to 3 per cent from 5. The government had to put even its embassy in Japan up for sale; thankfully, it didn't have to sell it finally. The country was near bankruptcy. It pledged twenty tonnes of gold to the Union Bank of Switzerland and another forty-seven tonnes to the Bank of England, as guarantee against bailout with the International Monetary Fund (IMF). India was also forced to go in for an economic reform because of the IMF bailout.

That is when the government decided to bid telecom licences in the metros.

Vivendi helped Sunil buy the Delhi licence. But when licences for the rest of the country opened up, Sunil didn't have the money to match the other bidders and lost the bids. This turned out to be a blessing in disguise. Within three years, it started becoming evident that most of his rivals had overpaid for the licences. They started losing money, and wanted to sell off their businesses, even at prices lower than their worth. Sunil was ready by then. '[I]n two or three years the other companies started falling like ninepins. They couldn't even pay the licensing fee. They struggled, and we were ready,' he told *Fortune* magazine.[3]

---

[3]Clay Chandler, 'Wireless Wonder: India's Sunil Mittal', *Fortune,* 17 January 2007.

The Mittal Way

Airtel kept growing stronger. In 1997, it became the first telecom operator to cross 100,000 subscribers. By March 2014, the number had exploded to 296 million (including Africa).

In 2002, Sunil had an epiphany. The subscriber base was doubling every year, and to stay ahead of the pack, he had to take his subscriber base to 25 million in the next couple of years—which meant huge investments in rolling out the networks, hiring people and expanding distribution and reach. He needed to employ anything between 10,000 to 20,000 people, including engineers, technicians and sales people. Could he afford that?

Sunil wanted to be like T-Mobile, Vodafone and Orange, but he didn't have enough money. So he decided to restructure the company in such a way that the cost per minute came down by ten times. Part of this was due to the suggestions of Akhil Gupta, managing director of the group and Sunil's close friend. In an interview with *Business Today*, Sunil said, 'Akhil said, "I want to buy minutes, I don't want to buy boxes." That is when we started this process on how to buy telecom traffic, not boxes.'[4]

Sunil is known to be radically different and a risk-taker. He says it is important to think transformationally, not incrementally. 'Technological changes in the environment keep creating numerous transformational possibilities for businesses/

---

[4]Josey Puliyenthuruthel, 'Sunil Mittal on Bharti Airtel's Telecom Entry, Africa Business and More', *Business Today*, 17 January 2012.

entrepreneurs. Such initiatives in one business/sector can trigger a chain reaction, creating endless possibilities,' Sunil opines.

A competent IT department was essential to manage the growing number of subscribers, but the best IT brains were going to firms such as TCS, Infosys, Wipro, IBM and Accenture. So Sunil decided to outsource his entire IT systems to IBM for $750 million over an eight-year period. It became an industry benchmark. Nokia Siemens Networks, Motorola and Ericsson, who had earlier built Airtel's network, were asked to manage it. The results were evident: by 2010, Airtel had 137 million mobile phone subscribers in India out of the total 500 million subscribers.

Even though he ventured into other areas of business, his telecom company continued to grow the fastest. Sunil began scouting for countries which had a similar market to India, with lots of opportunities. Africa was the perfect fit.

It's Time for Africa

In 2009, Sunil almost got what he thought was the golden goose of African telecom—MTN, Africa's largest telecom operator. He was in talks with MTN for a few months, but finally it didn't work out.

Six months later, he clinched the third-largest African telecom operator, Zain Telecom, in a $10.7 billion deal.

Why Africa? It has fifty-three countries, with a combined population of more than a billion, like India. Till then, the market was underpenetrated, data services were yet to take off and it was fragmented. Sunil saw an opportunity—he had enough learning from his India experience.

But he soon realized that even though Africa was like India, a lot still needed to be done differently at the local level. He had got a company with operations in sixteen countries in Africa, but Zain was running into losses. He had to fix that. He also had to align every operation and system in Zain so that it could be centrally monitored. The first thing that Sunil did was to build the infrastructure. It took him more than three years to get this right as every country there had a different infrastructural framework. He asked old Airtel hand, Manoj Kohli, to restructure the business in Africa and himself travelled there at least once every month.

'Think global, act local,' says Sunil. 'Markets can be unique to themselves and may exhibit surprising variations. No one model can fit all; adapting your business model to different market conditions holds the key.'

It has been almost six years since Bharti Enterprises bought Zain. Some of the bets are playing out now. In 2013-14, it earned a revenue of $4.9 billion, but growth is very slow. Sunil, however, feels that it is just a matter of time before his business in Africa will start making big money.

It was a big risk, as at the time the Indian business was registering decline in profits, quarter after quarter. At one point, Airtel's India profits kept skidding for twelve quarters in a row, mostly because of the massive price war started by the new telcos which were given licences in 2008. These new licences were later quashed by the Supreme Court, because of the 2G scam—where the Comptroller and Auditor General of India said that the process of issue of licences was faulty, and had resulted in a ₹173,000 crore national loss to the exchequer.

Soon, Sunil realized that the Indian side of business also needed to be revitalized. Internet usage was growing in India, most of it on mobile phones. Airtel had to change from selling just talktime to selling services—Internet packs, various schemes like Whatsapp @ ₹1 and low rates for Facebook, as well as a whole bunch of other services.

And to do everything, he always had the right people. 'Getting the right people at the right stage of organizational evolution' is his mantra. He understood that he needed someone in India who could make these products sell well and control, or even reduce, costs. So he got Gopal Vittal from Hindustan Unilever. Within a year, Airtel's profits started growing. Airtel closed the financial year 2013-14 at ₹85,746 crore of revenue and ₹2,773 crore of net profit.

It's not only about getting the right people, but also helping them think and work like entrepreneurs. Sunil says, 'There is an entrepreneur in each employee; empower them and let them discover their potential. Promote a culture of ownership of decisions across levels in the organization.'

The biggest factor which helped create a team of intrapreneurs within Airtel was the company's ability to be nimble-footed and non-bureaucratic. According to Sunil, 'You need to keep the fire of innovation and nimbleness burning. However, it is difficult to do so as you grow big and become structurally complex, saddled with inflexible systems and processes. Hence, maintain the heart of a small company.' Another advantage of thinking and operating like a small company is the positive effect it has on the interpersonal relations between employees, which, in turn, increases their engagement.

Today, Airtel is a huge conglomerate. Sunil has partnered with corporates from all around the world for his various ventures. For telecom, he collaborated with Emtel, Vivendi, British Telecom, Telecom Italia, Vodafone and Singapore Telecom. Mittal didn't know much about retail, so he partnered with Wal-Mart when the American retail giant wanted to enter India. He wasn't very knowledgeable about insurance, so he partnered with French insurance company AXA to launch Bharti AXA. Some partners gave him money, some gave him an understanding of how large firms work and some helped him in getting the best technology.

In his early years, Sunil had decided to retire at the age of fifty; that is now seven years overdue. But he loves what he does and has no reason to retire. The deadline has been extended indefinitely.

A Phone-man's Legacy | 93

SUNIL MITTAL'S MANTRAS FOR SUCCESS

No dream is too big.

Think transformational, not incremental.

Think global, act local. Markets can be unique to themselves and may exhibit surprising variations. No one model can fit all; adapting your business model to different market conditions holds the key.

Get the right people at the right stage of organizational evolution.

There is an entrepreneur in each employee; empower them and let them discover their potential. Promote a culture of ownership of decisions across levels in the organization.

You need to keep the fire of innovation and nimbleness burning. However, it is difficult to do so as you grow big [...] Hence, maintain the heart of a small company.

DEEPAK PAREKH AND ADITYA PURI

Deepak Parekh is the chairman of Housing Development Finance Corporation (HDFC). He has won many honours and accolades and was the first recipient of the Institute of Chartered Accountants in England and Wales' Outstanding Achievement Award in 2010. He has also won the Lifetime Achievement Award at the NDTV Profit Business Leadership Awards in 2012 and at *Businessworld's* Magna awards in 2014. Internationally, he was conferred the Cross of the Order of Merit by the Federal Republic of Germany in 2014. He was also awarded the Padma Bhushan in 2006.

Aditya Puri is the managing director of HDFC Bank. In 2014, under his leadership, HDFC was ranked the Strongest Bank in India on the Asian Banker 500 by balance-sheet ranking. Aditya Puri himself was conferred the award of Banker of the Year by *Business Standard* in 2013.

THE STORY OF TWO BANKERS

Deepak Parekh charted a new path for HDFC, turning it into a multi-function bank from a specialized mortgage firm. Aditya Puri is the astute banker who helped build HDFC into what it is today.

The year 1991 was a kind of inflection point for the Indian banking industry. The country's economy was opening up and new banking licences were being given out. The Housing Development Finance Corporation, or HDFC, was one of the new players to get a licence. After being founded in 1977, HDFC remained, for many years, a financial firm which only financed homes, as its name suggests. Now it was going to traverse an unknown path, and for that it needed a new head. In 1993, Deepak Parekh took over as the chairman of HDFC, from his uncle and the founder of HDFC, the legendary Hasmukhbhai Parekh.

The job of finding a banking head was entrusted to Deepak. In 1994, he travelled all the way to Malaysia to meet Aditya Puri and convince him to set up HDFC Bank. Aditya was then heading Citibank's Malaysian operations as its CEO, but a move was already on his mind. He wanted something more exciting and challenging. What was better than setting up a bank all by himself? Aditya agreed to join HDFC in the changeover journey. Eventually, HDFC's core business of financing homes became a small portion of its large portfolio of financial services. While Deepak became the custodian of the HDFC group, Aditya became the entrepreneur who changed its fortunes.

The Beginning

In the 1930s, when Hasmukhbhai was still studying at the London School of Economics, he had wanted to start an organization which would help Indians buy houses on mortgage, like people did in the West. Till then, for middle-class people buying a house was a difficult proposition—most of them bought it either after years of saving, in their late forties or fifties, or after they retired. Even Hasmukhbhai could only fulfil this dream of his after he retired from the Industrial Credit and Investment Corporation of India (ICICI), which is now HDFC's biggest competitor. Thus, in a way, HDFC was an offshoot of ICICI.

HDFC was started in 1977 with an initial capital of ₹10 crore. The visionary that Hasmukhbhai was, even at the time he would give loans based on the borrower's capacity to pay back, rather on the property's value. Later, all of HDFC's competitors began doing the same.

Within a year, Hasmukhbhai called upon Deepak, who was then

in his late thirties, and was working with Chase Manhattan Bank in Saudi Arabia. When he joined HDFC, he took a 50 per cent salary cut, but it was worth it. For years, HDFC relied on wholesale money that came from international agencies to fund its retail loans. It had no competition. Till the late 1980s, it governed 100 per cent of the housing loan business.

The next big opportunity for HDFC came in 1991, when the economy opened up. Deepak realized the need for HDFC to go into banking, but he needed someone who could do that for him. He found his man-at-arms in Aditya, who has been a banker for almost all his life.

The Other Banker

Aditya Puri, who had studied in Delhi, moved to Bombay to work under the finance director of Mahindra & Mahindra in 1975. He hated to travel from South Bombay, where he stayed in a paying-guest accommodation, to Kandivali, where his office was located. At the same time, Aditya envied his cousin who was working in Citibank, and was going off to Beirut for training. He soon applied to Citibank and got through. He, too, went to Beirut, often called the Paris of the East, where he had a good time. 'All I knew is that I had to work hard. If I continued and had a bit of luck, I would make it to the top,' he told Anand Adhikari of the India Today Group.[1]

---

[1] Anand Adhikari, 'Best CEO (BFSI): Aditya Puri', *India Today Group*, https://in.finance.yahoo.com/news/best-ceo-bfsi-aditya-puri-184200979.html, accessed on 2 January 2015.

From Beirut he travelled to Calcutta, and in a year's time moved back to Bombay. There he was shifted to a marketing profile, and soon became the country head of the wholesale business at Citibank. From there he went ahead to work with Citibank in multiple countries and finally ended up in Malaysia, where Deepak met him. Even at Citibank, Aditya was in the running to get a prestigious global position, but Deepak had luck on his side.

When Aditya joined Citibank, people told him that if he did not work late and schmooze with colleagues and seniors, he would never make it to the top. But Aditya was different. 'I thought about it and figured that if I have to do that and not go up based on calibre and hard work, then I would rather work for someone else. Fortunately, the impression people had on the mantra for success was incorrect because I *did* make it, while enjoying myself by living life on my own terms. So the moral of the story is: work efficiently during office hours and leave on time. Give the required time to family and friends.'

Even after so many years, this has not changed. He believes in only one thing: 'Having worked in some ten countries—Saudi Arabia, Greece, the UK, Malaysia, Hong Kong, Australia, etc.— one does realize that there is a need to have a professional, transparent and fair work style.'

Aditya was growing rapidly in his career, but one day after he came back home, he saw that his wife did not look very happy. A lot of people had told her that she would now have to accompany Aditya to his social and professional gatherings.

She did not want to be involved in his professional life. Aditya smiled and told her that he would be happy as long as she remained his pillar of support when he came back home.

Both Deepak and Aditya have a few beliefs in common—one being the need to empower people. Aditya believes that everyone should do their allocated jobs without over-interference from their seniors. 'I believe in empowerment rather than just delegation and…commanding respect on the basis of my knowledge and intellect rather than demanding it,' he says. His assessment of his employees is based on achievement of goals, transparency and being beyond reproach.

Deepak also follows the same principle, otherwise he would not have given Aditya a free hand to run the bank. 'Follow an open-door policy—a leader needs to be approachable and accessible… The age-old maxims of integrity, honesty and transparency will always stand the test of time… A good leader must also have a big heart and should stay humble,' feels Deepak.

Deepak is no longer involved in the day-to-day operations at HDFC. However, there were times when his involvement was paramount, especially during acquisitions. Deepak is a master at handling such mergers and under his watch, HDFC acquired Times Bank (2000), Home Trust (2000) and Centurion Bank (2008).

A Different Grooming

Deepak grew up in the corridors of banking, and banking was in his genes. The Central Bank of India had hired Deepak's grandfather as its first employee. His father, too, was an employee at Central Bank of India and retired as its deputy managing director. Deepak was earlier a chartered accountant in England, after which he worked for a few years in New York before returning to join his uncle's firm.

On the other hand, Aditya grew up in a family of air force officials, disconnected from the corporate world. While looking for work, he found that some of his friends who came from a corporate background had some 'pull' and got jobs more easily. 'I talked to my mother and she said—you have the greatest pull, provided you work hard,' he reminisces.

Aditya then asked her what this greatest pull was and his mother answered: God. He still believes that one should follow the teachings of age-old scriptures, work hard and live life honestly, leaving the rest to God.

Growing up in cantonments and shifting town every few years gave Aditya the ability to get along with different people as well as enjoy his own company. 'You learn to value teamwork, integrity, honesty and to love your country with all its faults,' he says. Even after working for so many years and being the highest-paid banker in the country, Aditya doesn't believe in the rat race. 'I am normally quite happy with myself. I also have interests in golf, music, gardening, trekking, good food, good wine and a good wife,' he says.

When he joined HDFC, he had a very clear vision—to build a world-class Indian bank. The upside was great. India, at the time, had 80 per cent of the market covered by public sector banks, which had the distribution and the money, but not the products and technology. The foreign banks, on the other hand, had the products and the technology, but did not have the distribution and the money. 'We picked the best of both worlds... We took advantage of discontinuities—the change that technology, computing and media brought in the way we work, play and live. Basically, geography was not important. Technology had become less expensive, premium was disappearing but not brand affinity, and so, if you had the best product at the best price with good technology and people, you were home,' says Aditya.

Aditya also decided to straddle India's gross domestic product, which is 55 per cent consumption and 45 per cent wholesale. So HDFC became the only bank with the same business mix—55 per cent consumer products and 45 per cent wholesale and market-related goods. Both Aditya and Deepak went about scouting for opportunities in semi-urban and rural India, which constitutes nearly 70 per cent of India's population. HDFC came out with offers tailormade for this segment. The duo also focused on virtual banking and used technology to provide a virtual experience which would in no way be lesser than the actual bank. 'This has involved use of data warehouse, customer relationships, system, repository, analytics, automation and digital marketing, and we believe we can match the best in the world,' says Aditya.

While Aditya made HDFC India's most valued bank, Deepak made HDFC a financial conglomerate, covering a gamut of financial services from house loans to financing institutions, from retail banking to mutual funds and insurance.

In the late 1990s, ICICI also entered the housing loan business. By then, learning from HDFC's practices, its competitors had progressed in the organized house finance business. But HDFC survived, and became India's most valued bank in 2012, surpassing State Bank of India (SBI).

Two things, Deepak says, helped them survive. 'HDFC was the pioneer in housing finance in India. There were no local models to emulate, so we adopted a "learning by doing" philosophy... Focus on creating a value-driven culture—HDFC was built on the principles of fairness, kindness, efficiency and effectiveness.'

At seventy, Deepak is still the non-executive chairman of HDFC, and the go-to guy in case of any crisis—and not just for HDFC. In April 2014, cricketing legend Sunil Gavaskar, who was the interim president of the Board of Cricket Control in India (BCCI), appointed Deepak as the special advisor for the Indian Premier League. At the time, the IPL was under a cloud of scandal due to allegations of spot-fixing. The BCCI press statement called Deepak the 'unofficial crisis consultant'. In 2009, when beleaguered IT firm Satyam had to be revived after a 7,000-crore fraud by its top honchos came to light, Deepak was appointed as a special director on the Satyam board.

Last Thoughts

For Aditya, life is like a river. There are obstructions along the way and one flows around them. While everything else is like a rubber ball and can bounce back, four things, he believes, are made of glass—family, friends, health and spirit. 'If you drop one of these, they would break and you've had it.' For him, it is important to live up to one's own expectations, not others'. 'I would like to close with a toast copied from one of my friends: "Here's to all who wish us well and the rest of the folks can go to hell".'

Deepak's idea of avoiding obstacles is more cautionary: 'Don't do anything that you'd be ashamed of were it to become public—there is no softer pillow at night than a clear conscience.'

Deepak and Aditya's winning combination has set standards for many banks across the country and their names are forever engraved in the history of Indian banking.

DEEPAK PAREKH'S MANTRAS FOR SUCCESS

Follow an open-door policy—a leader needs to be approachable and accessible...

A good leader must also have a big heart and should stay humble.

Focus on creating a value-driven culture.

Don't do anything that you'd be ashamed of were it to become public—there is no softer pillow at night than a clear conscience.

ADITYA PURI'S MANTRAS FOR SUCCESS

Work efficiently during office hours and leave on time. Give the required time to family and friends.

There is a need to have a professional, transparent and fair work style.

Work hard and live life honestly, leaving the rest to God.

Learn to value teamwork, integrity, honesty and to love your country with all its faults.

Everything else is like a rubber ball and can bounce back, but four things are made of glass—family, friends, health and spirit. If you drop one of these, they would break and you've had it.

I believe in empowerment rather than just delegation and...commanding respect on the basis of my knowledge and intellect rather than demanding it.

KISHORE BIYANI

Known as the 'Rajah of Retail', Kishore Biyani is the CEO of the Future Group, which has over 17 million square feet of retail space in 90 cities and 60 rural areas. His company received the Most Admired Food and Grocery Retailer of the Year at the Golden Spoon Awards in 2012 and the FedEx Most Trusted Retailer of the Year Award at the ET Retail Awards, also in 2012. He has also authored a bestselling business book, *It Happened in India*.

THE HOUSE OF MR BIYANI

Over the years, Kishore Biyani started some businesses, demolished others, sold some and bought more to create what is now the Future Group.

Kishore Biyani, founder and CEO of the Future Group, who is often called the king of Indian retail, lives by his beliefs. Given his humble past, to claw his way up to the top with no formal backing of big names would not have been possible without those beliefs, which he now calls his mantras.

Today, his Future Group has an annual turnover of ₹18,343 crore, even after selling Pantaloons, which was its flagship retail chain for the longest time. But like many other visionaries Kishore's beginnings were humble. His grandfather travelled from Rajasthan to set up a business in Bombay in 1935. He opened a wholesale shop in Vithawadi, in central Bombay, selling sarees and dhotis. Maybe that's where Kishore's liking for retail came from, through hearing stories about his grandfather.

After college, Kishore joined his family business, Bansi Silk

Mills. During the 1980s, he once saw one of his friends wearing stonewashed jeans. He then acquired the cloth from Jupiter Mills, a government-owned textile mill, and sold it in the open market to garment manufacturers.

That's when he got out of his father's shadow, tasted some success and made some money. Soon, he was selling to retailers as well.

It was time to let his dreams fly. In the early 1980s, he launched a brand of fabric for men's trousers, called WBB (White Blue Brown). After that, in 1985, he started selling men's trousers at a shop set up by him, called Patloon (the Urdu word for pant). On 12 October 1987, Kishore started a garment-manufacturing unit called Manz Wear Private Limited, and the garments were branded as Pantaloons, a derivative of Patloon. Pantaloons sounded like an Italian lifestyle brand, adding a touch of sophistication. In 1991, he opened the first Pantaloons store in Goa. Soon he started expanding, opening a host of small-format stores which would sell Pantaloons trousers. (Jeans brands like Lee and Levi's had not then taken off in India.)

Kishore now needed more money to expand. This was pre-liberalization, in the year 1992. He decided to go for an initial public offer (IPO). Pantaloons Retail was on the stock exchange and the listing, where 60 per cent of the company's stock was diluted, fetched Kishore ₹2.25 crore. He used up the money fast in opening many small stores, and soon got into a logistics problems. In his autobiography, *It Happened in India*, he wrote that he had spread himself very thin, because of which the business did not make profits.

He sometimes thinks it's not wise to force the pace. 'Go with the flow and never challenge the laws of nature,' he says. Around mid-1996, he thought of tweaking his existing business model by getting into large-format retail stores, selling apparel, electronics and food and groceries, and started scouting for locations for this. As destiny would have it, he was in Calcutta when he saw a 10,000 square feet property in Gariahat. He converted that into a large-format retail store. This marked Pantaloons' entry into modern retail. The year was 1997 and, at that time the biggest stores in the city were hardly half of Pantaloons' size. And this was just the beginning.

The Beginning

In 2001, Kishore opened the first Big Bazaar outlet in Kolkata and within twenty-two days he opened two more, in Abids, Hyderabad and Koramangala, Bangalore (now Bengaluru). Now, there are more than 100 Big Bazaars all around the country. In 2003, he launched Food Bazaar, which sold only grocery.

Kishore then launched a mall, Central, in Bangalore in 2004, and opened many more of these in other cities later. In 2006, he started a financial business, Future Capital Holdings Limited, that managed the $80 million (at the time) worth of real estate which the company owned, had a private equity to fund Kishore's new ventures and started retail infrastructure funds in the open market. In the same year, he entered into a joint venture with Italian insurance company Generali, and formed another joint venture with the US-based stationery major Staples. Home Town, furniture chain Furniture Bazaar, and electronics retail chain Ezone were also started in 2006. He also launched Fairprice, which was modelled on the next-door kirana store.

A year later, the group crossed its annual turnover of $1 billion. Its operations and business had spread so much that Kishore decided to bring in some supply chain and logistics experts. He entered into an agreement with Hong Kong-based Li & Fung Limited. Today, people who know him say that no other company in the offline space has perfected the supply chain and logistics as well as he has.

Kishore is known to take radical decisions, and one such decision was taken in 2008. He bought a 200,000 square feet property to open two separate large-format stores as part of his fast-paced retail expansion. Then the Lehman crisis happened and the world economy plunged.

He was in a fix. Bankers started calling in for the loans he had taken. He had to sell the mutual funds Future Group had invested in, and his sources of foreign capital were exhausted. Within six months, the company's market capitalization fell by two-thirds.

That was not all. His furniture retail business Home Town's sales went down by 30 per cent, making it a loss-making venture. Even then he asked his people to convert the 200,000 square feet into Home Town's flagship store. Most of them wondered what Kishore was up to, but he knew that the organized furniture business was yet to pick up. Two years later, the store made ₹200 crore in revenue, and proved that even furniture could be sold though organized large-format retail.

Not all of Kishore's dreams worked, however. In 2009, he also met Lars Olofsson, CEO of the world's second-largest retailer, Carrefour, but nothing came out of the meeting, according to *The National*.[1] But even though he might be interested in grabbing an opportunity with Carrefour, Kishore is inspired by Sam Walton, Wal-Mart's founder. A picture of him hangs on the walls of Kishore's office in Mumbai, which has the quote: 'Wal-Mart became Wal-Mart because ordinary people got together to do extraordinary things.'

The other picture that adorns the walls is that of Mother Teresa. The saint influenced Kishore a lot, to the extent that one of his mantras is 'to be a giver in life and not a taker', which he derives from one of Mother Teresa's famous sayings: 'Give till it hurts.'

Life after Pantaloons

The Future Group was financially in a bad shape, because Kishore's huge expansion plans hadn't worked out. He started slashing costs and streamlining his portfolio. He finally had to take the difficult decision to sell Pantaloons, his flagship business, to Kumar Mangalam Birla in 2012, to reduce the debt of the Future Group. When Kishore sold Pantaloons, it had more than 12 million square feet of retail space. But by then he had moved into other lucrative areas of food and groceries.

'Something I have learned from Indian ethos, beliefs and

---

[1]'The Making of India's Retail King', *The National*, 15 October 2009.

mythology—there is never an absolute right or wrong, truth or falsehood, saint or sinner, success or failure. Everything is subjective and needs to be judged based on the context,' he says.

At one point of time, Kishore, who used to shun consultants, even hired consultancy firm McKinsey to help him restructure the Future Group and get it back on the growth track. He also hired people from FMCG companies like Unilever and PepsiCo to run the day-to-day operations of the company. 'Be willing to always learn, unlearn and relearn,' he says. Perhaps this mantra is what made him let go the running of the daily operations of the company.

Kishore also overhauled the technology backend and brought in processes that drove efficiency and made the Future Group more transparent.

He also realized that buyers in India were different from those in the Western world. They were driven by ethnicity. No matter where a Bengali family travelled or, for that matter, a Malayalam or a Punjabi family, they rarely changed their eating habits. So he launched the brand Ekta, which focuses on ethnic food. Big Bazaar, however, continues to be the flagship and gets in more than two-thirds of the company's revenue.

Kishore also involved his daughter Ashni in the business in 2007. She led the strategic projects inside the group and played an important role in opening Food Bazaar Gourmet, which offers speciality food that caters to NRIs, foreigners and upmarket Indians who have developed a taste for gourmet delicacies.

Biting the Digital Bullet

In 2013, Kishore realized that he needed to take Big Bazaar beyond its current existence. The next thing was Big Bazaar Direct, which promised, in its teaser campaign, 'One lakh outlets, zero FDI. The future of FDI is coming soon.' Through a network of franchisees, Kishore wants to take Big Bazaar's merchandise to places where there were no Future Group stores. The franchisees would take orders on computers and tablets and these would be delivered to the customer's doorstep in three to seven days.

A pilot was started in September 2013 in Nagpur. Big Bazaar Direct still exists but the scale and scope of the venture is something that the company doesn't give out. Interestingly, this kind of home delivery of groceries has not taken off in India, but Kishore might just be able to turn it around.

Kishore is known to be a risk-taker and to flirt with new ideas. He wrote in his autobiography that he often dressed like a shopkeeper, plain and simple, and did things that his 'gut' told him was right. His role model is Dhirubhai Ambani, and much like Dhirubhai, he has built an empire in retail that others envy, including perhaps even Mukesh Ambani. Reliance Retail is Kishore's competitor, but on a much smaller scale. One thing which Mukesh doesn't do but Kishore is often seen doing is roaming outside his Big Bazaar outlets to see what works and what he needs to reinvent.

Kishore's newest vision is to take the Future Group to smaller towns and cities, which will give the company a bigger scale of operations and up its volume. One of his mantras is: 'Believe in oneself and in our country.' *The Hindu Business Line* reported that he and his brother bought distressed properties in Ujjain, Nanded and Indore.[2] The deals were done by Kishore's real estate company, Future Market Network, which runs malls for wholesalers, called World Market. Kishore is known to have bought these properties at lower prices than the market rate and will later convert them into malls, which he hopes will make money.

The latest trick up his sleeve is going into e-commerce. In the last two years, online shoppers have doubled to 25 million and the average daily growth in this sector is 150 per cent. E-tailing currently comprises 10 per cent of the organized retail market and is expected to reach 25 per cent in the next few years, according to a CRISIL report. Kishore could not afford to miss this opportunity. After blaming e-commerce firms for undercutting prices during Diwali to destroy competition, his Future Group partnered with American e-commerce giant Amazon's India arm. He had earlier announced that he would invest ₹100 crore in Omni (multi-channel) retailing. The partnership between the Future Group and Amazon is expected to bring a lot of synergies in distribution, lead to cross promotion and acquire more consumer eyeballs. Kishore's goal is for the Future Group to become a $20 billion company by 2020.

Kishore Biyani does not believe that he created the company

---

[2]Priyanka Pani, 'Biyani Bets on Retail Story in Small-town India', *The Hindu Business Line*, 16 June 2014.

alone. 'There is never one element that makes an idea, business or individual successful. It is the coming together of multiple things that brings about success,' he says. But he has definitely created a legacy in the retail sector that is here to stay.

KISHORE BIYANI'S MANTRAS FOR SUCCESS

Go with the flow and never
challenge the laws of nature.

Be a giver in life, and not a taker.

There is never an absolute right or wrong, truth
or falsehood, saint or sinner, success or failure.
Everything is subjective and needs to be judged
based on the context.

Be willing to always learn, unlearn and relearn.

Believe in oneself and in our country.

There is never one element that makes an idea,
business or individual successful. I
t is the coming together of multiple things
that brings about success.

PAWAN MUNJAL

Pawan Kant Munjal is the managing director and CEO of Hero MotoCorp Limited, the world's largest manufacturer of two-wheelers since 2001. He is responsible for the growth and strategic planning of the Hero Group. He was awarded the Business Leader of the Year at the AIMA Managing India Awards 2013 and the NDTV Profit Business Leadership Awards in 2012 and 2013 (in the Automobiles [Two-Wheelers] category). In 2012, his company got the Best Value for Money Bike Maker and Best Advertising awards at the Auto India Best Brand Awards.

THE REAL HERO

His father established the Hero Group in India, but Pawan Munjal has taken Hero MotoCorp across the world.

One motorcycle jumped out of a sand dune and another motorcycle seemed to almost drop from the sky. The year was 2010 and the month was February. Pawan Munjal, CEO and managing director of what was then Hero Honda, had taken 1,200-odd dealers, vendors and employees to Dubai to see the spectacle, which was nothing less than a stunt fiesta. Actually, the company was showcasing its nine new products.

Huge projectors had been put up all around, showing images of the new products. 'It was the company's marketing convention, and the razzmatazz was unparalleled,' wrote Alokesh Bhattacharyya for *Businessworld*.[1] Earlier that year and the year before, competitors Bajaj Auto, Yamaha and TVS Motor had either launched new products or done facelifts of

---

[1] Alokesh Bhattacharyya, 'Entering the Rough', *Businessworld*, 10 May 2010.

their existing ones. But the trade needed reassurance from Hero Honda, and there was no better way to do it than a sort of a carnival for dealers in Dubai. After all, Hero Honda's market share was also grand—it sold six out of every ten motorbikes in the Indian market, which made it the leading two-wheeler maker of the country by a huge margin. In 2009, Hero Honda sold 3.7 million two-wheelers, most of which were bikes. It had even widened its lead over its arch-rival Bajaj Auto. Pawan has always maintained that capturing the market requires a lot of hard work, and that's the magic behind the company's success.

Hero Honda started out as a joint venture between Hero Cycles of India and Japan's Honda Motor Co. Ltd in 1984. The partners announced their split in 2010, after twenty-six years. At the time, Hero Honda was the country's largest two-wheeler maker, and the second-largest two-wheeler maker in the world. In fact, Hero Honda had also by then become the world's largest motorcycle manufacturer. At the time of the split, both Hero and Honda held an equal 26 per cent stake each in the company; the rest was held by external investors. Later, Pawan bought Honda's share, and Hero Honda was promoted by him alone. He had the option of continuing with the earlier name till 2014, but in 2012, he renamed the company Hero MotoCorp.

All of this sounds grand, but its beginnings were humble and difficult.

Ludhiana to London

The Munjal family's original business, till 1944, was of vegetable trading in a small town called Kamalia, now in Pakistan. The family soon shifted base to Amritsar. There, Pawan's father, Brijmohan Lall's elder brother decided to get into trading bicycle components. The problems of Partition forced them to shift to Ludhiana, where they came in touch with some artisans from the Ramgarhia community, who made fine cycle components. The Munjals used their financial strength and marketing prowess to sell these technically superior tools.

The aftermath of World War II had left India almost devastated, with hardly any industrial machinery. After Independence, Prime Minister Jawaharlal Nehru invited entrepreneurs to set up new infrastructure and create wealth. Brijmohan travelled across the country looking for new entrepreneurial avenues. One such opportunity lay in making cycles. Within no time, he set up Hero Cycles, which is now run by Pawan's cousin, Pankaj Munjal. The youngest of Brijmohan's four brothers, Om Prakash Munjal, was entrusted with the responsibility of establishing a national distribution network. Brijmohan even started travelling to other countries to understand how to use better technology for manufacturing cycles.

Apart from the Munjals, other business families such as the Birlas, with Hind Cycles, and TI (Tube Investments) Cycles in southern India entered the trade. But the Munjals knew it better than the others, because of their extensive market research and their previous business of cycle components. Within seven years, Hero Cycles became the country's largest cycle maker.

In the early 1980s, Pawan joined Hero Motors. He saw his father sign the iconic Hero and Honda deal in 1984. Brijmohan didn't want to make motorcycles—India was majorly a scooter market—but Honda had already inked a deal with the Firodias of the Kinetic group to make scooters. Within months, the company launched its initial public offering (IPO), and the first assembly line to manufacture the 100cc CD 100 bike came up in 1985. Sixteen years later, in 2001, under Pawan, Hero Honda overtook Bajaj Auto to become India's largest two-wheeler company. 'Envision a world that is unimaginable and then go about changing it. But whilst doing so, hone the ambition with strong implementation processes,' says Pawan, who learnt this from Brijmohan.

What also worked in Pawan's favour was Rajiv Bajaj, the head of Bajaj Auto, shifting focus from 100-125cc bikes to more powerful ones. While people aspired for the Pulsar, they usually ended up buying bikes with lower power, which would be cheaper as well. By then, Pawan had already launched the Splendor, which broke all records to become the world's largest-selling motorcycle. Their Gurgaon plant produced a motorcycle every eighteen seconds. The 70-acre campus, where visitors were taken around in golf carts, showcased Japan's technological prowess.

'I have always believed [that] at the heart of technology is humanism. Create products that will always have an emotional connect. Create products that will help your customers smile and be joyous. Give them service that doesn't just satisfy them but instead, delights them,' says Pawan.

Pawan learnt a few other things from Brijmohan as well, such as rural distribution. When Brijmohan started making bicycles, a large part of the sales came from the rural segment. But with the motorcycle business, the concentration was more in towns and cities. When the economic downturn hit in 2008, Hero Honda's growth stagnanted. Pawan figured out that there was an opportunity to boost sales in the hinterland. He created a separate sales division which only monitored rural sales. He also kicked off a campaign where he set a mandate that Hero executives would cover 'every village, every home'. Today, the company dealers have a field force of 500 rural sales executives.

The implementation was fast, and the results were soon visible. For example, in a village called Mansar Kheri, near Jaipur, with only 3,300 inhabitants, there are 300 Hero bikes. The village chief alone has four Hero bikes! Hero's rural network is so deep-rooted that other rivals, including Bajaj Auto and Honda Motorcycle & Scooter India Pvt. Ltd (HMSI), haven't yet been able to beat them. It has become Pawan's recipe for success.

But success brings with it its own problems. Fissures in Hero and Honda's partnership had started forming in 2001 when Hero Honda became the number one two-wheeler company by sales volumes in the world. A year later, it became the first Indian company to cross the sales mark of 7 million units. Honda's partnership with Kinetic was over, and so it decided to launch in the Indian market on its own. It came out with scooters like Activa, which made a huge impact on the market.

On 16 December 2010, the stock market was informed about the split. There was panic all around; Pawan's phone didn't stop ringing as inquisitive journalists, trade and equity analysts, and component makers tried to understand the situation. But Pawan was more worried about his employees and dealers. Hero Honda was dead overnight, and dealers believed that the move would kill their businesses as well. However, what followed not only gave them confidence, but also cast a glimpse into what was to come in the next few years.

The day after the announcement of the split, Pawan did a live webcast with all his employees, vendors and dealers. Bhupesh Bhandari in *Business Standard* wrote,

> The next day, the key hundred or so dealers were brought to Delhi, and the father-son duo apprised them of the situation. Within ten days, each one of the 100,000 or so mechanics and salesmen of the dealerships and the 4,000-odd touch points (service centres et cetera) were given dockets on the subject, and their questions were answered by the company's employees. Close to a year later, Hero MotoCorp claims not a single dealer left it, in spite of the doomsday projections.[2]

Even though the Munjals could use the Honda name on their products for another four years, Pawan thought he should finalize the split at the earliest. In August 2012, Pawan took about 1,300 dealers, employees and vendors to London and Hero MotoCorp, as the company is known today, got its new identity. A function was held to mark the occasion at the Millennium Dome or O2 Arena, on the southern bank of the Thames.

---

[2]Bhupesh Bhandari, 'A New Hero', *Business Standard,* 5 November 2011.

A.R. Rahman created a jingle to grace the occasion.

Though the divorce was amicable, and Brijmohan and Pawan had kind words to say about Honda, it led to problems of the kind that the Munjals had never faced before. They had always worked in partnerships, so Hero had hardly any resources for technology and R&D. Creating these was Pawan's biggest challenge. After all, now there were more people looking at Pawan through a magnifying lens.

Life after Honda

Before working on an R&D department, Pawan had to see to it that the sales were better than in the partnership days. He called his senior leadership team and asked for ideas to revive the flattening sales. This was in early 2013. One of them suggested that the warranty for all Hero products should be increased to five years from two. No one in the industry had done so before. It took Pawan just four days to implement it. This was in complete contrast to the time when the partnership was still alive, when it would take a long time for anything to be actioned. For example, the discussions between Hero and Honda to set up a plant in Haridwar went on for three years before arriving at a decision. Now the Haridwar plant is Hero MotoCorp's biggest one, producing 9,500 motorcycles per day.

Earlier, Hero was only involved in minor tweaks in the products, while all the processes were laid out by the Japanese partner. But since the split, the number of engineers at Hero MotoCorp have doubled to more than 400. The company has also entered into a series of partnerships with other firms—Erik Buell Racing (EBR) of the US to make speciality heavy engines (Hero MotoCorp has even acquired 49.2 per cent of EBR); a joint venture with Italy's Magneti Marelli to make powertrain components; another with Italy's Engines Engineering for technology for mass-market motorcycles; and finally with Austrian firm AVL to develop engines based on both the new platform and the older model. Hero MotoCorp has already launched its first indigenously developed motorcycle.

While Pawan believes that ideas are everywhere, it is more important to provide a space that will help in better ideation and implementation. 'Ideas belong to no one. So create an environment where an idea can emanate from anyone. It could be the person on the shop floor or the person who is in the R&D department or from people who don't know your product but know what they seek,' he says.

For ideas and R&D, Kukas, near Jaipur, is where the Hero campus is spread across 250 acres. The main R&D building is almost at the centre of the plot, standing 12 storeys tall.

Miles to Go

Once Honda had parted ways, it was also time for Pawan to look beyond India. For years, due to the partnership, Hero Honda was confined to the Indian subcontinent (apart from India, it could sell only in Nepal, Sri Lanka and Bangladesh). Pawan has a wider canvas to play on now: 'Borders are meant for nations. Not for products. So whenever you think of doing something, benchmark it not to your own country but to the world. Make your brands globally the best and not just local heroes.'

In the last four to five years, Hero MotoCorp has already made inroads into close to fifteen new geographies and there are plans to go into fifteen more. Pawan plans to grow Hero MotoCorp's overseas presence to a dozen countries in the next four years, and expand its sales to 10 million units.

Pawan has chosen his markets very strategically. He is not going into the US or China, but targeting areas where there is demand but the penetration is low, and which resemble the Indian market in some ways. He has gone to Central American countries like El Salvador, Honduras and Guatemala; South American markets such as Peru, Ecuador and Colombia; East African countries like Kenya, Mozambique, Tanzania and Uganda, where there are factories; and has set up distributors in Burkina Faso, Angola and the Ivory Coast in West Africa.

To understand the pulse of the market, Pawan says it's important to be a good listener. 'Only good listeners make for great managers. Listen with your soul and your mind—with everything at your command. Listen all the time. Because only then will you be able to respond with care and responsibility.'

Within a short span of time, Pawan has taken audacious steps and achieved targets that very few can dream of. Even without Honda, he rules the roost at the Indian motorcycle market.

PAWAN MUNJAL'S MANTRAS FOR SUCCESS

Envision a world that is unimaginable and then go about changing it. But whilst doing so, hone the ambition with strong implementation processes.

I have always believed [that] at the heart of technology is humanism. Create products that will always have an emotional connect. Create products that will help your customers smile and be joyous. Give them service that doesn't just satisfy them but instead, delights them.

Ideas belong to no one. So create an environment where an idea can emanate from anyone.

Borders are meant for nations. Not for products. So whenever you think of doing something, benchmark it not to your own country but to the world. Make your brands globally the best and not just local heroes.

Only good listeners make for great managers. Listen with your soul and your mind—with everything at your command. Listen all the time. Because only then will you be able to respond with care and responsibility.

ANALJIT SINGH

Analjit Singh is the founder and chairman of Max India Limited, a $2 billion company. He is a director on the boards of several leading companies such as Tata Global Beverages and Sofina NV/SA, Belgium. He is the chairman of the Confederation of Indian Industry (CII)'s National Committee on Insurance and Pension; the board of governors of the Indian Institute of Technology (IIT), Roorkee; and the Max India and Bhai Mohan Singh foundations. He was awarded the Padma Bhushan in 2011, Ernst & Young Entrepreneur of the Year in 2011 and the Golden Peacock Award in 2012.

THE COMPULSIVE ENTREPRENEUR

Analjit Singh's life can be divided into two halves—in one, he got the wrong end of the stick but didn't give up and in the other, he not only made money but also built a healthcare conglomerate whose byword is quality.

Analjit Singh lives in a mansion on Aurangzeb Road in Lutyens Delhi, which would easily cost a few hundred crore rupees. He loves dogs, and believes in businesses that revolve around health and wellness. With a net worth of more than $700 million, he recently stepped down from the active role of chairman of the Max India group, which had an annual revenue of ₹9,139 crore in 2013-14.

This is a far cry from how he started out. Despite his father, Bhai Mohan Singh, being a wealthy industrialist (he owned the pharmaceutical firm Ranbaxy), Analjit did not have it easy. In 1989-1990, Bhai Mohan Singh split the family business between him and his two elder brothers, Parvinder and Manjit. While his brothers got the Ranbaxy business and the family real estate, all Analjit got was a rundown factory in Okhla where he had to pay voluntary retirement money to many of his employees from his own pocket. The seeds of this unequal split had been laid much earlier.

The Beginning

After finishing his master's degree in Business Administration from Boston University, Analjit returned to India and incorporated Max India in 1982. He had initially joined Ranbaxy in 1981 but his stint there was short-lived because of the unsatisfactory distribution of the business and wealth between him and his brothers.

At Ranbaxy, he had been the director of an upcoming penicillin project in Punjab, but after quitting, he started out with something that had nothing to do with pharmaceuticals or healthcare. It was Dove Corporation, which sold premium liquor and fashion labels in duty-free shops. Soon the business started making money. In 1985 Max India started its operations. One of its ventures was packaging films. But because of the Gulf War, the packaging films' business started running into losses.[1] Max India had started supplying penicillin to Ranbaxy as well but after the final split between the brothers, Ranbaxy stopped sourcing from Max. Analjit's business almost shut down.

He now had to look for other options. At the time, telecommunications was at the bottom of the curve but poised

---

[1] Ranju Sarkar, 'The Evolution of Analjit Singh', *Business Standard*, 9 November 2011.

to take off. Motorola was a leader in the manufacture of pagers the world over. Analjit tied up with Motorola to offer radio paging services, but soon realized he was sailing in the wrong boat. Partnering with a hardware provider was not advisable as there was a chance that the device would become obsolete. So he decided to retreat and enter into a joint venture with Hutchison Telecommunications instead. His decision proved correct: three decades later, Motorola has been sold off, though the brand still exists.

On 21 February 1992, Analjit partnered with Hong Kong-based Hutchison Telecommunications to launch cellular services in Bombay under the name Hutchison Max Telecom Ltd. He knew that the mobile industry would grow exponentially and again, he was right. Within six years, the company's operations in Mumbai alone was valued at ₹1,368 crore. Analjit could have stayed on in this, but Hutchison did not want to expand outside Mumbai because of regulatory uncertainties and high licence fees. So Singh sold and exited that business too. He made ₹561 crore by selling 41 per cent stake in the company back to Hutchison and to Kotak Mahindra. Recently, Analjit also made news once again, when he sold his remaining 24.65 per cent stake in Vodafone India (the latest avatar of Hutchison Max Telecom Ltd) in April 2014 for ₹1,241 crore. As always, he exited some businesses to get into others.

Cut back to 1999. By now Analjit had exited about eight- to ten-odd businesses. He used a sum of ₹200 crore, gained from those exits, to open up the first Max Hospital and simultaneously build a health insurance business. 'Don't look to decide your life's projects and journey in one week. The journey will be assembled over a lifetime. You will find the projects and they will find you,' he says.

Analjit had finally started something that he would build and fashion into his own brand, a sustainable business which we know today as the Max India group. The group owns hospitals; provides life insurance (in collaboration with Japan's Mitsui Sumitomo Insurance Group); health insurance (with the UK's Bupa Finance Plc); has a fully owned research clinic, Max Neeman Medical International; and a senior citizens' community, Antara Senior Living, which is run by his daughter Tara Singh Vachani.

However, all of Analjit's problems didn't end. In 2006, when Bhai Mohan Singh died, Analjit's and Parvinder's family got into a bitter, property-related family feud, which was lapped up by the Indian press. Finally, telecom czar Sunil Bharti Mittal helped sort matters between them after several meetings on both sides.[2] Relations are peaceful now, and Analjit has finally inherited a few of his family's prime properties in Delhi, after another round of bitter battles with his other brother Manjit.

These events left Analjit a little wiser. He wants the group to be promoter-governed but not promoter-managed, as he told *Forbes* in 2011.[3] Even the entire family real estate is now taken care of by a trust, headed by a team of trustees. 'Even if I suddenly go mad and do something crazy, the independent

---

[2]Megha Bahree, 'Family Feuds', *Forbes*, http://www.forbes.com/global/2008/0616/054a.html, accessed on 28 December 2014.
[3]Prince Mathews Thomas, 'Analjit Singh's Future-Proof Strategy', *Forbes India*, 18 April 2011.

trustees have the veto power to override my decisions,' he said.

Analjit is not in favour of his children running the family business by virtue of just being born to it. He believes one should earn the power. Perhaps that is why he is helping his children establish their own companies, and not making them directly part of his healthcare and insurance businesses. Nonetheless, he believes that, under certain circumstances, it is good to have a promoter-led company: 'In India, we are besotted with the promoter. If you are a publicly listed company or a company active in areas concerning the public, you are at best a sponsor.'

In 2009, Analjit told *Outlook Business* that he had the option of divesting all his businesses and retiring.[4] He would have definitely led a luxurious life with all the money he had made. But he decided to continue.

It took Analjit eighteen years to start building something which would live beyond his time—the Max businesses. But, like he says, 'There is no shortcut to doing the right thing and doing it right. Failure is the subtracted portion or the gap in this approach. Pay now or later. Reap always later. That is business. That is life.'

Eye for Detail

Even though Analjit started much ahead of his nephews, Malvinder and Shivinder Singh, the owners of Fortis Healthcare

---

[4]Ashish Gupta and Anurag Prasad, 'The Two Lives Of Analjit Singh', *Outlook Business*, 28 November 2009.

Ltd, Max Healthcare is much smaller in size than Fortis, with just eleven hospitals. It is also smaller than the Apollo Hospitals group, owned by the Reddy family. But Analjit is not worried. 'This is a focus yuga [era],' says Analjit. 'We will achieve what we focus on. So make sure you focus and if so, then on the right goal.' He is a micro-manager, and likes to get updates on anything which has gone wrong in the group within thirty-six hours. He cannot keep an eye on everything if his businesses become behemoths. He is even known to choose the furniture for his office and hospitals.

Analjit has implemented a lot from his experience. When he went to other hospitals, he did not like the smell of disinfectants. So in all Max Hospitals he has ensured that there is a small coffee-vending machine on the left, near the entrance. The aroma of the coffee is better than that of a disinfectant, he feels. 'If no one orders a coffee in 10 minutes, a cup of coffee is brewed and drained down. As a result, you always get an aroma of coffee when you walk into any Max Hospital,' Analjit told *The Economic Times*.[5]

The same news report mentioned that in Max Hospitals, when a patient is given food, the attendant never turns his back while leaving the room, keeping in mind that the patient might not be in a position to call the attendant if he needs something. It is also important to have eye contact with the patient always. In the case of life insurance, too, the agent and the policy holder's interactions are measured throughout the life cycle of

---

[5] Moinak Mitra, 'How Max India Chairman Analjit Singh's Penchant for Quality Service Defines his Work Culture', *The Economic Times*, 28 June 2013.

the policy, because Analjit believes that there are various changes that a person's life goes through, and Max should touch the client at every stage. All these are collectively summed up in the Max quality system.

In 2010, Analjit hired Prashant Hoskote as the head of quality and performance excellence. Prashant had spent many years as a consultant-cum-trainer for companies such as the Taj Hotels, Standard Chartered and Mashreq Bank. Prashant told *The Economic Times* in 2013 that when Analjit met him he asked, 'Why is it that when someone from another large company walks into my office and I receive him, without even knowing which company he represents, I almost know which group he belongs to? So why don't I see that common mindset, that common management language, that common improvement thinking in my organization?'[6]

That question remained with Prashant as he took up his task. In 2010, board meeting discussions at Max were about businesses, finances and strategies, but no one talked about quality. Although every company in the group had a quality head, there was no synergy between them and the quality heads never met. They all met for the first time at the first quality meeting after Prashant joined in 2010. After a series of brainstorming sessions with them, a framework was created, called the Max Performance Excellence Framework (MPEF), an outcome of the amalgamation of five global quality models—Japan's Deming Prize, the US's Baldrige Model, the European Foundation for Quality Management, the Australian Business

---

[6]Ibid.

Excellence Framework and the Singapore Quality Award. A fifty-page feedback form was created, which is now directly sent to Prashant, and after five days of rigorous exercise, an MPEF score for each company is derived. This score is a part of the key result area (KRA) of every company CEO. MPEF is now part of the Max DNA. The group has also implemented global processes like Lean Six Sigma in a few of their hospitals. This has brought down discharge time by 75 per cent.

None of this would have been possible without the right team, and Prashant is just one of Analjit's key lieutenants. 'Build the best team you can. One can't do it on one's own. The market, the world, is too complex,' says Analjit.

When Analjit put a governance structure in place in an attempt to strengthen the board, he took help from three people—management guru Ram Charan, Anuroop 'Tony' Singh and Ashwani Windlass. Tony and Ashwani are his childhood friends. Ram Charan now has direct access to Analjit's three children and they often meet to discuss a range of issues from their responsibilities as owners, recruitment and the success of their companies to how to work with the other board members. Tony, who was the founding CEO of Max New York Life, at one point wanted to move on and pursue the role of being an independent director. But Analjit managed to persuade him to stay back.

After a point, maybe Analjit realized that his people, at least at the top level, could never be fully empowered as long as he was at the helm. Therefore, in April 2014, he stepped down from the position of executive chairman to focus on planning and strategy, and handed over the daily running of the group to Rahul Khosla. Rahul is now the managing director of Max India and chairman of Max Healthcare. Another key person is Mohit Talwar, the deputy managing director of the group.

For Analjit, and for the Max India group, this is not the end but only the beginning. He sums up his mantra for life pretty neatly: 'If you die on a Monday and if five people miss you on the following Friday, you have done something brilliant. Live life. Lift the game. Be honest. Let go.'

ANALJIT SINGH'S MANTRAS FOR SUCCESS

Don't look to decide your life's projects and journey in one week. The journey will be assembled over a lifetime. You will find the projects and they will find you.

There is no shortcut to doing the right thing and doing it right. Failure is the subtracted portion or the gap in this approach. Pay now or later. Reap always later. That is business. That is life.

This is a focus yuga. We will achieve what we focus on. So make sure you focus and if so, then on the right goal.

Build the best team you can. One can't do it on one's own. The market, the world, is too complex.

If you die on a Monday and if five people miss you on the following Friday, you have done something brilliant. Live life. Lift the game. Be honest. Let go.

KIRAN MAZUMDAR-SHAW

Kiran Mazumdar-Shaw is the chairperson and managing director of Biocon Ltd, India's leading biopharmaceutical company, which has partners and customers in over seventy-five countries. She was included in *Time* magazine's 100 Most Influential People in the World in 2010. She is the founder-member and current chairperson of Karnataka's Vision Group on Biotechnology, and a member of several government bodies, including the General Body of the Indian Pharmacopoeia Commission. She has received many honorary degrees and prestigious awards, including the Padma Bhushan in 2005.

THE HEALER

Kiran Mazumdar-Shaw's appetite for taking risks, married with innovation, led to the making of Biocon Ltd.

In 2002, Nilima Rovshen was diagnosed with breast cancer. For six years, Kiran Mazumdar-Shaw took care of her. They had been best friends for decades. Nilima would recover, but the cancerian pincers would always pull her back—notwithstanding the number of chemotherapy and radiation sessions she underwent.

Finally, cancer did get the better of her in 2008. Neither the treatment (including complete brain radiation therapy just before her death), nor Kiran's nursing helped. Nilima died two months after she went on a vacation to Spain with Kiran.

Perhaps it was this that spurred Kiran's quest to make a homegrown cancer-treating drug. The irony is that today, she is the founder, chairman and managing director of Biocon, a billion-dollar biotechnology pharmaceutical company based out of Bengaluru, which recently manufactured a cancer-treating drug. With a net worth of over $655 million, according to *Forbes*, she is India's richest female entrepreneur. But despite all that, she couldn't save her best friend.

Money can't buy lives, but at times it does save many. And Kiran did have enough to save her husband's life later.

Just one year before Nilima died, Kiran's Scottish husband John Shaw was diagnosed with renal cell carcinoma, more commonly known as cancer of the kidneys. Unfortunately, India had few places where John could be treated and Kiran had to take her husband to London.

Nilima's death and then John's diagnosis did two things. Kiran realized the importance of psycho-oncology, a branch that treats the social, psychological, emotional and other day-to-day aspects of cancer. It was hardly practised in India, and she wanted to do something about it. She also decided to develop a cancer-treating drug, a dream that she shares with her husband, who is the vice-chairman of Biocon.

The first was easier—Kiran partnered with long-time friend Dr Devi Shetty, owner of Narayana Hrudayalaya (now Narayana Health), to open a cancer research centre.

The second one wasn't as smooth. Manufacturing a home-grown drug isn't easy when all the international pharma companies are pumping in billions of dollars in research to make the next wonder drug. But Kiran rose to the challenge, taking up a new project to create a made-in-India cancer drug in 2007.

Seven years later, in 2014, Biocon announced a breast-cancer treating drug that is 25 per cent cheaper than its nearest competitor in the global market. Herceptin, the other such drug by Swiss pharma major Roche, had global sales of $6.4 billion and sales in India of $21 million in 2012.

Kiran says that building competitive advantage is one of her success mantras: 'Driving sustainable growth through building continuous competitive advantage is a strategy I have encouraged in the organization. Be it new technologies, intellectual property or scale, we have successfully created value by focusing on competitor complacency.'

The Brewer's Daughter

When Kiran was young, her father worked in the liquor industry, which always embarrassed her. After all, in the 1970s, the liquor business was not thought of as a 'clean' profession. However, her father managed to convince her that brewing was a science, although that did not make her lean towards the profession. After school, she wanted to study medicine, but fell short of the qualifying marks for the medical entrances. Her father refused to pay a donation for her admission. So she decided to study zoology, and later went to London University for a PhD in genetics.

While in London, she decided to take up brewing after all and moved to Australia to the University of Ballarat to study the industry. She came back to India and applied for a job, but the liquor industry still had a bias against women. Even while studying the science, she had been the only girl in her class.

'I felt let down. It seemed to me that the success at Australia was just a veneer. Below it, the bottom was meant to fall. That was the reality,' she told *Forbes* magazine[1].

But fortune favours the brave. An Irish chemical company, Biocon Biochemicals Ltd, was looking for a partner in India to set up an enzymes business and Kiran, who had learnt the art of mixing in Australia, signed a joint venture with them.

That is how Biocon was created—out of a garage, with a seed capital of ₹10,000, on 29 November 1978. Kiran was then only twenty-five years old. In about a year, Biocon became the first company to export enzymes to the US and Europe. Eventually, Unilever became her biggest client.

Kiran says, 'As a pioneer, I have understood the power of differentiation to build leadership. I have always chosen to lead rather than follow. This has created tremendous brand leadership.'

In 1989, Biocon became the first company to get funding from the US for its proprietary technologies. Unilever wanted the company to continue in the field of enzymes. But Kiran was restless; she wasn't ready to make enzymes for the rest of her life. What next?

In 1996, using her experience from the enzymes business and the technology Bicon had created over two decades, she ventured into biopharmaceuticals. Soon enough, the fact that Biocon had started with the business of enzymes would get buried in articles and newsprints. 'I have always believed in challenging the status quo and have benefited exponentially by reinventing

---

[1]Subroto Bagchi, 'How to Bottom Out', *Forbes India*, 11 September 2009.

the business every five to seven years,' says Kiran.

Healing the World

Biocon's early days were a struggle for Kiran. There was no venture capital funding, loans were available only at high interest rates and it was the time of the licence raj, when, people joked, one required a licence even to own a bathroom. But above all, in those times, a woman starting a business was unheard of. She had to create a company that would generate its own revenue and be sustainable.

The first drug Biocon came out with was human insulin (a drug for diabetic patients). Later it joined hands with Pfizer, one of the world's leading insulin makers. In October 2011, it also launched the InsuPen, an injector used to take insulin.

After that, Biocon started working on oral insulin (separately from Pfizer), which again had a big market, as many people did not like to take insulin injections but were okay with popping pills. 'We are already the world's fourth-largest insulin producer and on our way to becoming the third largest, once our Malaysian insulin facility goes on stream in 2015,' says Kiran.

For manufacturing biosimilars products (medical products whose active drug substance is made or derived from a living organism) Biocon joined hands with Mylan, a generics and speciality pharma company. While generic drugs were getting commoditized, there were not many firms in the biosimilars business—globally, about ten-odd. Kiran chose three areas of focus: autoimmune diseases, cancer and diabetes.

Companies then did not invest much in technology. They would either buy it or spend very little in developing it. Kiran struck gold in this area. Even in bad times, Biocon invested as much as 7 per cent of its revenue into R&D, whereas global majors only spend up to 4 per cent. Of course, global companies have more revenue.

Kiran concentrated on a hybrid model—to go after the low-hanging business, which has little risk, is predictable and has a lot of scale. That makes up the larger chunk of Biocon's revenue and, Kiran says, generates enough cash to built newer businesses, like making a drug. 'I have long understood that leadership is about global scale and have invested strategically in building this. Today, we have [a] recognized global scale in fermentation-based bulk drugs and insulin production,' she says.

Biocon is already India's largest diabetes' drug-maker, and the fifth largest globally. Insulin alone has a worldwide market of about $25 billion. And in cancer drugs, Kiran sees an opportunity of more than a billion dollars.

Husain on the Wall

Biocon's 20-acre campus reveals Kiran's idea of scale, her eye for detail and her involvement in everything she does. The office is wood-panelled, surrounded by palm trees—designed for comfort. Inside the building, where her husband's room is next to hers, there are innumerable memorabilia—from pictures with eminent dignitaries and politicians, including one with US President Barack Obama, to framed certificates of honorary doctorate degrees—from the University of Glasgow in Scotland, Trinity College in Ireland and the University of Ballarat in Australia.

In an interview with *Mint*, Kiran said that she had designed her office keeping in mind that it should be homely and comfortable, as she would spend a lot of her time there.[2] Her love for artefacts, sculptures and paintings is evident. One of the most prominent paintings there is by the late M.F. Husain, and there is another by Yusuf Arakkal. The rest of the office space is full of awards.

It was in 1983, just five years after she started Biocon, that Kiran bought this campus as a part of a distress sale. She always knew she could not continue in a garage for long and needed to scale up. It was a calculated risk, like the ones she took when she decided to get into biopharmaceuticals from enzymes, and products from generics.

Even her decision to go for an initial public offer (IPO) in 2004 was a calculated risk. At the time, while IPOs were getting strong investor traction, Biocon was still transforming from an enzyme-maker to a medicine-maker. Aware of the risks, Kiran went ahead with the IPO. The stock got oversubscribed thirty-three times. 'The ability to manage and mitigate risks and failures provides us a competitive advantage and prevents both reputation and business impact,' she believes.

---

[2] Aparna Pirmal Raje, 'The Adaptable Innovator', *Mint*, 9 December 2012

Desk from the Garage

There are some things Kiran will never discard, like cards and letters from her old friends. But perhaps the most notable object is her working desk, which has been with her since her start-up days. While the desk remains, everything around it changed. She says she is sentimental about it.

Kiran retains old things and builds on top of them. An example is how, in the early days of Biocon, she decided to venture into patented enzymes from industrial enzymes. Industrial enzymes were easier to make, while for the former, she had to innovate on the existing technology.

Again, when Biocon ventured into pharmaceuticals from enzymes, Kiran used her learning from the latter and applied it to the former. Later, once her pharma business started doing well, she used the learning of developing generic drugs to create special drugs that would cater to emerging countries and were low cost. One of her biggest creations was the breast-cancer drug.

Innovation has many forms, and one of them is applied innovation (a term used by Vineet Nayar, author of *Employees First, Customers Second*), which means to keep on adding to the existing product to build new ones. Biocon is a classic example of applied innovation.

Kiran takes a lot of pride in talking about this, and it ranks second in her list of success mantras: 'Innovation has been my hallmark and we have consciously built a creative culture across all levels of the organization. We have a large and diverse portfolio of patents that has built a strong value base for the organization that is being periodically monetized.'

In hindsight, she would have liked to create the drug much earlier. Nilima Rovshen had had to import a lot of her medicines, which drained her financially. But there are more reasons to be happy now. Every time Kiran's husband completes his biannual check-ups and the reports are clean, she celebrates.

In a man's world, Kiran Mazumdar-Shaw created Biocon. She has often said that while many of the industry greats are visionaries, she isn't one of them. She had a mission: to build a biotech company that would make a mark on the global map, and would change the world's perception that India wasn't capable of creating a research-based company. Today, Biocon is a billion-dollar company.

And of course, Kiran's mother, Yamini Mazumdar, who was diagnosed with cancer a few years back, was treated at the Mazumdar-Shaw Cancer Centre. Some of Kiran's dreams may have come true, but there are many more ahead.

KIRAN MAZUMDAR-SHAW'S MANTRAS FOR SUCCESS

Driving sustainable growth through building continuous competitive advantage is a strategy I have encouraged in the organization. Be it new technologies, intellectual property or scale, we have successfully created value by focusing on competitor complacency.

As a pioneer, I have understood the power of differentiation to build leadership. I have always chosen to lead rather than follow.

I have always believed in challenging the status quo and have benefited exponentially by reinventing the business every five to seven years.

The ability to manage and mitigate risks and failures provides a competitive advantage and prevents both reputation and business impact.

Innovation has been my hallmark and we have consciously built a creative culture across all levels of the organization.

P.R.S. OBEROI

Prithvi Raj Singh Oberoi is the executive chairman of the board of East India Hotels Ltd (EIH) and the chairman of Oberoi Hotels Pvt. Ltd, the majority stakeholder in EIH. Widely considered to be the founding father of modern luxury hospitality in India, he was awarded the Padma Vibhushan by the Government of India in 2008. He was also conferred with a Lifetime Achievement Award at the CNBC TV 18 India Business Leader Awards 2007, followed by another at the Ernst & Young Entrepreneur of the Year Awards 2008. The Oberoi Group owns and/or operates around thirty hotels across six countries under the brands 'Oberoi' and 'Trident'. Many of its hotels have received prestigious awards. The group is also involved in other services such as car rentals, in-flight catering, and travel and tourism.

THE ERA OF A HOTELIER

Prithvi Raj Singh Oberoi brought luxury into Indian hotels, but there is a lot more he should be credited for.

On 26 November 2008, visionary hotelier Prithvi Raj Singh 'Biki' Oberoi was ecstatic as he received a Lifetime Achievement Award at the Ernst & Young Entrepreneur of the Year awards, held at the Taj Lands End in Mumbai. In less than an hour, though, his happiness was replaced by shock and dread as news of militants attacking various places in Mumbai spread. Out of the places which were attacked, two were Biki's hotels—The Oberoi and Trident.

Biki was almost in tears. He stayed at the Taj Lands End through the night, glued to the television screen, as the carnage continued. The siege lasted for a full three days. Thirty-two people were killed in both his hotels; around 166 died in total.

'We were affected severely [...] the attacks happened and Bombay emptied out,' recalled Biki in an interview to

The New York Times[1]. It took one month to reopen Trident, which had not suffered much damage, but The Oberoi was in bad shape. For Biki, this was the opportunity to not only redo the hotel and give it a more contemporary look, but also to send out a strong message to the perpetrators of terror. It took four months of planning and eleven months of reconstruction to make the hotel shipshape again.

Though the newer property essentially looked the same, Biki managed to make enough changes to alter the character of the palatial complex. Apart from overhauling the hotel's security apparatus, the new property was soundproofed by using double-glazed panes; the suites were redone to make them roomier (some of them by combining rooms); the seating in the lounge was also redone; and the coffee lounge was turned into the Champagne Lounge (with Dom Pérignon now being stocked there). A new restaurant, Ziya, also came up, managed by Vineet Bhatia, a former Oberoi chef who had found great fame in the UK.

Biki, the chairman of EIH, the holding company that owns The Oberoi Group, oversees an empire of more than thirty hotels and luxury cruisers. A lot of what he learnt was from his father, Rai Bahadur Mohan Singh Oberoi, the founder of The Oberoi Group. Mohan Singh was more of a businessman and less of a hotelier, but a true creator nonetheless.

---

[1] Vikas Bajaj, 'Mumbai Hotel, a Killing Zone, Is Grand Again', *The New York Times*, 20 April 2010.

Passing the Baton

Mohan Singh was born in India in 1898. His father died when he was just six months old, so he led a life of struggle. He went to Shimla, then the summer capital of British India, in search of a job. There, he joined the front desk at Hotel Cecil, which he later acquired. The manager at Cecil, Mr Ernest Clarke, bought the Carlton Hotel in Shimla (renamed Clarkes), which he wanted Mohan Singh to manage. Later, Mohan bought it by mortgaging his wife's jewellery, to start his own venture. The year was 1934.

Four years later, Mohan signed a lease to run The Grand Hotel in Calcutta. The hotel had been up for sale after a cholera epidemic broke out in the city in 1933, resulting in the deaths of many of its guests. Initially, it was difficult for him to convince people to come to the hotel, but once they did, they became regulars. He was also given the title of Rai Bahadur in 1941 by the British.

Over the years, Mohan Singh also kept accumulating shares until he got a controlling stake in Associated Hotels of India, which owned the Cecil and Corstophans hotels in Shimla, the Maidens and Imperial hotels in Delhi, as well as properties in many other cities. So, in 1943, he became the first Indian to run the largest chain of India's finest hotels.

Biki Oberoi didn't have to go through any such struggle. His father asked him to travel far and wide, experience the best hotels around the world, stay in them, eat at the best restaurants and drink the best wine in Rome, Paris, London, New York,

Tokyo, etc. till the age of thirty-two. This would help him understand the art of service better, and would be the pillar of Biki's success. 'To achieve excellence in any field, one needs dedication and passion,' he says. And he showed both the qualities in abundance.

It was then time to get down to serious business. In 1954, Biki was put in charge of the Maidens Hotel in Delhi. Fifteen years later, the group became the first Indian hotel brand to open a property outside the country, in Nepal.

By then, the group had already ventured into modern luxury with the opening of The Oberoi in New Delhi in 1965, which marked the beginning of a new era of luxury hotels in India.

Biki admires Regent Hotels' founder Robert Burns, from whom he learnt the Western style of service. The other hotelier he admires is Isadore Sharp, founder of the Four Seasons Hotels and Resorts. There are two things that Biki thinks are important, which are also his success mantras: 'The devil lies in the details' and 'Successful organizations consider people as their most important asset'.

The Devil and the Asset

In the early 1970s, no Indian property was in the list of the world's top hotels. Mohan Singh told Biki that they needed to improve the standard of their hotels by many notches. So Biki started with the people. Great service would be at the core of his luxury hotels, and for that he needed a well-trained staff—something he would get from an institute he had already established. In 1966, he had opened The Oberoi Centre of Learning and Development, at a time when subjects like hotel management were alien concepts in India. 'Never leave tasks for tomorrow which can be dealt with today,' he says, a mantra which might have been the reason to open up an institute so ahead of its time. Now, a hundred students graduate from this institute every year. Biki makes sure he is present in the final interviews for selection. Having a staff comprising the best people in the hotel industry has helped him a bit more than others. *Business Today* once reported that a guest staying at an Oberoi sees the hotel staff forty-two times in the course of a day, giving the staff ample opportunity to decipher the individual preferences of each guest.[2]

The Oberoi Vanyavilas in Ranthambore, The Udaivilas in Udaipur, The Amarvilas in Agra and The Rajvilas in Jaipur have, over the years, ranked as the best hotels in the world, with price tags that are jaw-dropping, some going into multiple lakhs for a suite! The group has also gone international in a big way, with properties in Dubai, Egypt, Mauritius, Indonesia and Saudi Arabia.

Guests at an Oberoi hotel have an experience like none other. The group has created an outstanding database. For example, if someone checks into an Oberoi once and orders a particular flavour of tea, the hotel will make sure that the same flavour is available every time the guest checks in. The database has details of each one of over 11 lakh people who have stayed at Oberoi hotels. This helps Biki observe the spending pattern

---

[2] Manu Kaushik, 'Guest Star: The Oberoi', *Business Today*, 5 September 2010.

and push promotional campaigns that would be of interest to prospective guests.

Biki's love for detail can be seen in the fact that he goes through every architectural plan, every design that goes into his hotels. He has a say in every little thing—the height of the ceilings, the size of the rooms and even the design of the furniture. He chose the marble for redoing The Oberoi in Mumbai. His ingredients for Japanese dishes come all the way from the Tsukiji market in Tokyo.

Raymond Bickson, former managing director and CEO of Taj Hotels, Resorts and Palaces, told *Hotels* magazine in 2010 that Biki is a visionary. 'Biki has always stood for excellence and quality in whatever he does... He has been an inspiration for many Asian hoteliers.'[3]

Over the years, The Oberoi Group has been pushed to the number three position by the Taj group and the ITC Hotels, but Biki is unfazed. 'We don't want to be in the quantity race. Quality is our focus,' he told *The Times of India* in 2011.[4] But in the last couple of years, he has talked about getting more aggressive. There are about a dozen new Oberoi properties which either have just been completed or will come up in the next few years. This includes a hotel in Gurgaon, in Hyderabad, as well as in cities all over the world such as Marrakesh, London, New York, Shanghai, Moscow and Paris. 'Always look towards the future and not the past,' says Biki, who thinks it's never

---

[3]'Hoteliers of the World', *Hotels*, November 2010.
[4]Reeba Zachariah and Shubham Mukherjee, 'Luxury for Oberoi is "Just a Perception"', *The Times of India*, 30 April 2011.

too late to tweak his business model, as long as he can make it relevant for the future.

The Oberoi of Tomorrow

Mohan Singh died in 2002 at the ripe old age of 104. He saw The Oberoi Group become one of the most luxurious hotel chains of the world.

Now, the third generation of the Oberoi family is waiting in the wings, and it is likely that Biki's son Vikram will be his successor.

Vikram isn't as flamboyant as his father. He did not get to travel around the globe like Biki did. Once, he saw a cigarette butt lying near the entrance of The Oberoi in Delhi and instead of asking any of the staff members, picked it up himself and threw it in a bin.

Biki trained his son in a different way than his father had done for him. While kids his age enjoyed their vacations, Vikram always spent his summer holidays at his father's hotels, training. In between, he did flirt with an alternate profession as a stockbroker in McCaughan in Australia, but in 1991 he was back and took to the hotel business built by his grandfather and father wholeheartedly.

Maybe Biki foresaw the future of the hotel industry, which lies not in opening more properties, but managing them for others. So, in order to take on the business of tomorrow, Vikram needed to carefully understand every operation. Vikram has had stints in almost every unit of a hotel, be it reception, travel desk and even housekeeping. In the late 1990s, Biki made Vikram the general manager of The Rajvilas in Jaipur. Taking over the palace and turning it into a hotel was considered by many as risky. Some even said that it would see its end even before it started operations. But against all odds, The Oberoi Rajvilas is a jewel in Biki's crown and has won many global awards, including *Gourmet's* Most Exotic Resort in the World.

Biki wanted Vikram to learn the ropes from scratch, perhaps because he believed that Vikram should have his own decision-making abilities. Therefore, he was made the chief operation officer of the group. After all, this is one of Biki's success mantras: 'Take advice from others but ultimately trust your own gut.'

The Oberoi Group is up against tough rivals—international and Indian chains, once Biki's mentors, are closing in on his business, including the Four Seasons and the Ritz Carlton. But Biki seems unruffled. Time and again, he has managed to make the right type of investments, without diluting the core aim of the group, that is, treating its customers to high-end luxury.

Biki Oberoi is now eighty-four. He still has to make a few winning strikes to end his era. He has already stated his vision for the next decade: 60 per cent of the hotels' portfolios that the group will have then will be solely managed by them, not directly owned. That's where the business is moving, globally. Right now, 80 per cent of the properties are owned by the group.

On the personal front, Biki has already thought about retirement. If he does, he will move out of his home, Villa Aashiana—on the outskirts of Delhi on a 55-acre land—to stay in Nandi Hills, 35 kilometres from Bengaluru, where he has built another Oberoi nest. Maybe he will also find more time to paint, a newly acquired hobby. But for now, he doesn't want to hang up his boots.

When he does, Vikram will have a tough legacy to uphold—the legacy of a hotelier par excellence.

P.R.S. OBEROI'S MANTRAS FOR SUCCESS

To achieve excellence in any field,
one needs dedication and passion.

The devil lies in the details.

Successful organizations consider
people as their most important asset.

Never leave tasks for tomorrow
which can be dealt with today.

We don't want to be in the quantity race.
Quality is our focus.

Always look towards the future and not the past.

Take advice from others but ultimately
trust your own gut.

SANJIV GOENKA

Sanjiv Goenka is the chairman of the RP-Sanjiv Goenka Group, India's youngest business group with an asset base of over $4.3 billion that has businesses in sectors such as IT and education, retail, media and entertainment, power and natural resources, carbon black, and infrastructure. Sanjiv is also the chairman of Woodlands Medical Centre Ltd, Kolkata, and on the board of IIM Kolkata. He was the youngest-ever president of Confederation of Indian Industry (CII) and chairman of the board of governors of IIT Kharagpur.

WALKING IN HIS OWN SHADOW

Sanjiv Goenka's first independent business decision was buying an underperforming power company in 1989 and turning it around. He now runs his own business conglomerate, the RP-Sanjiv Goenka Group.

In the seventeenth century, Calcutta was an important commercial hub for India. The British established a base there for the East India Company. It even served as the capital of India until 1911, when the capital was shifted to Delhi.

After Independence, Calcutta's commercial activity continued with companies like Shaw Wallace, Brooke Bond, Philips, Ispat Industries, Bata and Britannia, which had their headquarters in the city. But with the rise of the labour movement and mass strikes in West Bengal, especially in the 1960s, very few companies chose to stay back. The Goenkas were among them.

The Goenkas

In 1820, Ramdutt Goenka arrived in Calcutta from a small town in Rajasthan, with dreams of doing business with the East India Company. In the course of the next hundred years, the Goenkas grew enormously. The big transition happened in 1950, when Ramdutt's great-grandson Keshav Prasad Goenka bought two British trading houses—Duncan Brothers and Octavius Steel. In 1979, Keshav's son Rama Prasad Goenka (better known as R.P. Goenka), established RPG Enterprises with Phillips Carbon Black Limited (PCBL), Asian Cables, Agarpara Jute Mills and Murphy India as its constituents. The 1980s saw further acquisitions by the group, the first being CEAT Tyres in 1981. The group then went on to acquire Searle India, now RPG Life Sciences (1983); Dunlop (1984); Gramophone Company of India Ltd, now Saregama India (1986); and finally, Harrisons Malayalam, Spencer & Co. and Fujitsu, ICIM (now Zensar Technologies) all in 1989.

Business was in Sanjiv Goenka's blood. Like his father, R.P. Goenka, who built his empire through a series of takeovers, Sanjiv bought his first company when he was only twenty-eight years old. That was the Calcutta Electric Supply Corporation (CESC), a private power company founded in 1897 (then known as The Indian Electric Company Limited), which supplied electricity to Calcutta and its surrounding areas.

In 1989, C.K. Dhanuka, now an independent director with CESC, wanted to sell the shares he held in the electric company and approached R.P. Goenka, who rejected the offer. The reason was simple—the company was no more a relevant power supplier as it had failed to increase its power generation capacity after Independence. Due to this, over time, Calcutta had become infamous for its long power cuts. For R.P. Goenka, CESC did not have a future. Sanjiv, though, saw an opportunity. He went against his father's advice and bought the company.

Doing business in Calcutta wasn't easy for Sanjiv. The early days were especially nightmarish as CESC employees were opposed to the takeover and showed their displeasure blatantly. One morning, when Sanjiv reached Victoria House, the headquarters of CESC, he saw his effigies being hung in front of the office. He was perturbed but decided to take the challenge head-on. For the next decade, he put in all he had to resurrect CESC. He lobbied with the state government to raise power tariffs. Alongside, he added more capacity and gave his employees direction. He tried to instil in them a sense of pride in working with a company which had heritage. 'One should lead by example, in thought and action,' feels Sanjiv.

Cut to Financial Year 2013-14—CESC's sales stood at ₹5,510 crore and net profit at ₹652 crore. This turnaround is nothing less than phenomenal when compared to 1989, when the revenue was only ₹300 crore, and net profit was around ₹5-6 crore.

Labour problems are now a thing of the past. In fact, within five years of buying CESC, Sanjiv was able to reduce head count by 3,500 and there wasn't a single protest, something unheard of previously in West Bengal. Over the years, Sanjiv's faith in Kolkata has grown stronger.

Sanjiv now owns businesses in six sectors, with over fifteen companies and more than 55,000 employees. 'It's been a very interesting journey, filled with lots of challenges, not the least that of getting the team at CESC to rally behind me, to work with me, and to respect me,' he told *Business Today* in 2011.[1]

Out of RPG's Shadow

In 2010, R.P. Goenka officially divided RPG Enterprises between his sons, Sanjiv and Harsh. Harsh, who had moved to Mumbai by then, got the tyre company CEAT, the power engineering company KEC International, IT firm Zensar Technologies and pharma company RPG Life Sciences. Sanjiv got CESC, Noida Power, Integrated Coal Mining Limited (ICML), retail businesses Spencer's and MusicWorld, music company Saregama India, carbon black manufacturer PCBL, Au Bon Pain Café India, media company Open Media Network and the real-estate company CESC Properties.

The Goenka brothers had an amicable split and even today they don't have any non-compete agreement. Sanjiv believes they do not need that because they are, after all, the same family, with the same inheritance and same legacy. 'We can enter each other's businesses, though we may not like to do it, given the emotional bonding,' he said to *Business Standard* in 2011.[2]

In 2011, Sanjiv renamed his group the RP-Sanjiv Goenka Group. At that time, he also made clear his intentions of

---

[1]Somnath Dasgupta, 'Shining in His Own Light', *Business Today*, 21 August 2011.
[2]'Sanjiv Goenka Steps out of RPG Shadow, Carves out New Identity', *Business Standard*, 14 July 2011.

expanding to other parts of the country. He ventured into Maharashta—CESC's first power project outside West Bengal—to build a 400-KV transmission line in Chandrapur that got commissioned in 2013. There are two more proposed power projects in Pirpainti, in the Bhagalpur district of Bihar, and Neulapoi, in the Dhenkanal district of Odisha. Sanjiv has also taken CESC to the state of Jharkhand, where it won a licence to distribute power in 2012, and is setting up projects in Noida, in the National Capital Region, as well. The group's coal mining firm ICML produces 3 million tonnes of coal every year. In Asansol, West Bengal, ICML has commissioned a coal washery. Sanjiv is also coming up with a coal thermal power project in the port town of Haldia in West Bengal.

Powering Ahead

CESC, which was almost dead and buried in the 1980s, is now the group's flagship company. PCBL is the country's largest carbon black manufacturer. Over the years Sanjiv has started many more new businesses. Some of them are still small, but he believes that he has placed his bets right and he already has his support system ready to carry on his dream.

'Identify five to six operating issues facing each company for every quarter and focus on them,' is Sanjiv's driving principle.

In 2011, as the world was coming out of a global recession and retail chains like Subhiksha were closing down, Sanjiv's retain chain Spencer's Retail got into trouble too. Some of the stores had to be shut down, a conscious decision taken by Sanjiv to maintain profits.

Spencer's has an illustrious history. It had been started in 1863 by John William Spencer and was spread across undivided India. It was even present in Karachi in Pakistan and Chittagong in Bangladesh at the time. In 1989, it was acquired by the RPG Group.

'There are some stores which are perennially loss-making. Most of those have been closed down. But now we have to take a call (on viability of each store relative to the back end),' said Sanjiv to *DNA* in 2012.[3]

The latest addition to Sanjiv's kitty is Firstsource. When he secured a controlling stake in this business process outsourcing company, it was in high debt. Sanjiv took what is called the baniya approach—cutting costs and wastages and focusing on profitability. In two years' time, the debt equity ratio went down to 0.3:1 from 1:1.

Sanjiv also owns *OPEN* magazine, that competes with the likes of *India Today* and *Outlook*. Its presence might be smaller than these top magazine brands, but its content is highly appreciated.

Sanjiv is, by far, one of the most successful businessmen of eastern India, but he is quick to credit his success to others. 'I may be ordinary but I like to be surrounded by extraordinary people,' he says. That might be true to an extent, but when he placed his biggest bet, of buying CESC against his father's

---

[3] Sumit Moitra, 'Spencer's Goes Ruthless on Store Viability', *DNA*, 8 December 2012.

wishes, he didn't have anyone else. It was the conviction he had that spurred him to do so, and with that conviction he has gone ahead to build an empire very few would have dared to, in the city of Kolkata.

SANJIV GOENKA'S MANTRAS FOR SUCCESS

One should lead by example,
in thought and action.

Identify five to six operating issues facing each company for every quarter and focus on them.

I may be ordinary but I like to be surrounded by extraordinary people.

K.P. SINGH

Kushal Pal Singh is the chairman of Delhi Land and Finance (DLF) Ltd, India's largest real-estate company. He was ranked the richest real-estate baron and the eighth richest person in the world by *Forbes* magazine in 2008. He led a movement for self-regulation and ethics in the real-estate industry, which lead to the formation of the National Real Estate Development Council (NAREDCO), part of the central government, and the State Real Estate Development Councils (State REDCOs) in various states. He was awarded the Padma Bhushan in 2010.

THE MAN WHO CREATED GURGAON

Real-estate king Kushal Pal Singh had a meteoric rise when he gave birth to what people know as Gurgaon today.

One decision could have changed Kushal Pal Singh's life forever. In his autobiography, *Whatever the Odds: The Incredible Story Behind DLF*, he writes that when he was at the Indian Military Academy, he'd wanted to run away to England. He wrote a long letter about his escape plans to his friend Julie who lived in England, and dropped it at the letter box in the academy. Hardly a few hours had passed when he was summoned by Lt Col Baljit Singh, the battalion commander. His letter had been intercepted before being sent.

Lt Col Singh first offered to help Kushal escape from the academy. But he also said that if Kushal stayed in England he would always remain a nobody and if he came back to India, he would be called a bhagora, a runaway. 'It was my first lesson in brilliant man management. Had he reprimanded me sternly in the typical army way and threatened me with dire consequences, I would have probably quit. Instead, he used warmth and advice to get me to think the way he wanted me to,' writes Kushal in his book.[1]

After graduating from the academy, Kushal joined the Deccan Horse—a cavalry regiment headed by General M.S. Wadalia. Wadalia was so impressed by Kushal that he recommended him as a potential groom to his friend Chaudhary Raghvendra Singh for his daughter Indira.

The Beginnings of DLF

DLF, was started before Independence, in 1946, by Chaudhary Raghvendra Singh, who had earlier served in the army, to cater to the large demand for housing in Delhi after the influx of refugees as a result of the Partition in 1947. He developed no fewer than twenty-one colonies in Delhi between 1947 and 1957, including commercial and residential spaces like South Extension and Greater Kailash. But after 1961, all development in the capital was taken over by the Delhi Development Authority (DDA).

After marrying Indira, Kushal quit the army and joined his father-in-law's business. Raghvendra Singh made him go through the grind. He had to work with other DLF companies like Willard India and American Universal Electric Company—

---

[1] Kushal Pal Singh with Ramesh Menon & Raman Swamy, *Whatever the Odds: The Incredible Story Behind DLF,* HarperCollins, 2011.

which made fractional motors, and was an unprofitable business. Finally, in the early 1980s, DLF moved back to real estate. Kushal also exited other DLF businesses which weren't doing well. For example, DLF Cement, a 1.5 million-tonne plant, was sold to Gujarat Ambuja for ₹142 crore.

Perhaps Kushal always knew this was the only solution. 'Focus on the essentials. Come to grip with the minutest details. But don't ever lose sight of the big picture. Keep your eye on the ball. But always be aware of the rest of the field,' he says.

Before opportunities knocked at his door, Kushal had almost sold his shares in DLF in 1975 for the meagre amount of ₹26 lakh. DLF was facing problems because of the strict government regulations. It was a difficult decision not to give in as it was a huge amount back then. But he stuck to his guns and went on to become India's richest real-estate mogul, worth $35 billion at the peak of DLF's value, according to *Forbes*.

When Kushal developed DLF City in Gurgaon, Haryana, the company had been out of the real-estate business for almost two decades.

The Millennium City

By the late 1970s, Delhi's home and office spaces had started becoming expensive. Till then, Gurgaon in Haryana was more or less the back of beyond. It had got separated from Faridabad in 1979. Faridabad was developed by its municipal corporation, while Gurgaon remained rural, where the chief minister's office directed the acquisition and development of land. Most of the land in Gurgaon was held by members of the Ahir community, who were traditionally farmers.

Kushal had seen the opportunity to develop Gurgaon, but to convince the farmers to sell their land was the most difficult task, as it was something they had inherited from their forefathers. He spent months and years discussing it with them over cups of tea, and multiple glasses of milk and buttermilk. Soon, he even found himself settling family disputes, getting their children into schools and even promising to arrange ten times more land for them, which would be fertile, as against the barren lands they then owned. 'Identify with the people who work with you. Learn how to earn their respect. Encourage them to get along with each other,' is his motto.

He eventually acquired 40 acres of land from these farmers, in the hope of getting the permissions to develop it. In 1981, DLF became the first company to get a licence to develop land in Gurgaon. This was primarily due to the efforts of Kushal. However, serendipity played a big part in DLF's success as well.

One of Kushal's most famous stories is about how he first met former Prime Minister Rajiv Gandhi in 1981. It was on a hot summer afternoon, when Kushal was in Gurgaon. Rajiv Gandhi's jeep pulled up by the side of the road, and he asked Kushal for water as the engine was overheating. In the conversation that followed, Kushal told the Prime Minister about his dream of creating a modern city on the outskirts of Delhi.

The PM seemed taken by Kushal's idea and asked what was holding him back. Kushal said that the land laws were such that private players could not develop. Kushal and the PM sat there for more than an hour-and-a-half, and discussed land regulations and town-planning regulations and statutes.

Once Kushal got the permission from the government, he decided to develop the entire land on his own and not outsource it to any other developer. 'Take decisions only after getting to the heart of the matter by studying the issue deeply. But the trick lies in not getting immersed in details so much that you cannot separate the meat from the bone,' is his mantra.

The 40 acres which DLF had bought has now become part of DLF City, a large expanse of land spread over 12 square kilometres. Kushal has developed Gurgaon into a business district full of towering glass-fronted buildings, occupied by firms both national and international. He knew that if people went to work in Gurgaon, they would need places to live in, as well as other amenities close by, so DLF also built residential areas, restaurants, hotels, shopping malls and hospitals. Kushal thus became the chief orchestrator of DLF's success and scale and DLF City is his masterpiece. As he says, 'Corporate decisions have to be based on a judicious blend of both the macro-picture and the micro-reality.'

Rise to the Top

The next big breakthrough for DLF had come in 1983, when Kushal managed to obtain permission to develop 556 acres of land close to the first Maruti Suzuki plant, writes Praveen

Donthi in *The Caravan* magazine[2].

In 1989, Kushal met Jack Welch, the iconic General Electric (GE) CEO, who was scouting India to open a back-office centre for GE. He also set up a meeting between Jack and Rajiv Gandhi, and another one for Jack with Azim Premji, as GE was also looking to partner with someone for its healthcare systems business. Jack liked Gurgaon and set up GE's back office there. He mentioned in an interview later that Kushal played an important role in GE's entry into India.[3]

DLF Corporate Park was where GE Capital International Services (GECIS), a fully owned subsidiary of GE, was born. (Later, it came to be known as Genpact, now India's largest BPO). At that time, Gurgaon was hardly connected to Delhi. There were no restaurants or hotels in Gurgaon either. But after GE came, Gurgaon and Kushal quickly got a bunch of other big names in. Ericsson, American Express, IBM, PepsiCo and Nestle were just a few of the many MNCs which started offices there.

DLF's tagline is 'Building India'. From the very first day the Government of Haryana decided to start planning, developing and initiating projects in Gurgaon, Kushal was there to offer his advice. As Praveen Donthi mentions in *Caravan*: 'When National Highway 8 was being built, for example, the company successfully lobbied to have the route brought closer to one

---

[2] Praveen Donthi, 'The Road to Gurgaon: How the Brokers of Land and Power Built Millennium City', *The Caravan*, 1 January 2014.
[3] 'K.P. Singh Almost Sold DLF Stake for ₹26 Lakh', *Business Today*, 15 November 2011.

of its townships, it claims on its website. (It did something similar when the metro was being extended south from Delhi, according to news reports.)'[4]

'Stretch the rules if you have to, but do not ever break the law,' says Kushal. 'Look for the silver lining behind every dark cloud.'

After the office complexes and the residential complexes came up, the population of the city boomed. Kushal's marketing of his residential complexes as 'walk-to-work' proved successful. In ten years, starting 2001, the city's population grew by 75 per cent to 1.5 million.

In 2007, thanks to Gurgaon's rapid growth, it was time for DLF to raise more capital. The real-estate company managed to raise ₹9,200 crore through the largest initial public offer (IPO) in India. Of course, as Kushal grew, he surrounded himself with the best people. His children Pia and Rajiv too joined the business. 'Avoid verbosity. Be precise. Surround yourself with people of robust common sense,' he believes.

Kushal wielded so much power at one time that DLF even coined a new term 'New Gurgaon' for the areas and the building projects developed by its rivals, like the Mumbai-based real-estate companies, the Rahejas and Hiranandanis, and the Ansals.

Presently, both DLF and Kushal have run into problems. However, people who know Kushal well are confident that he will bounce back. 'Everybody makes mistakes. Everyone has failures. Try to learn from them. Treat them as opportunities to

---

[4]Praveen Donthi, The Road to Gurgaon: How the Brokers of Land and Power Built Millennium City', *The Caravan*, 1 January 2014.

begin again more intelligently,' he says. Everyone knows that when times are bad it is important to run a tight ship but according to him, 'Practise austerity even in times of prosperity.'

KP SINGH'S MANTRAS FOR SUCCESS

Focus on the essentials. Come to grip with the minutest details. But don't ever lose sight of the big picture. Keep your eye on the ball. But always be aware of the rest of the field.

Identify with the people who work with you. Learn how to earn their respect. Encourage them to get along with each other.

Take decisions only after getting to the heart of the matter by studying the issue deeply. But the trick lies in not getting immersed in details so much that you cannot separate the meat from the bone.

Corporate decisions have to be based on a judicious blend of both the macro-picture and the micro-reality.

Stretch the rules if you have to,
but do not ever break the law.

**Look for the silver lining
behind every dark cloud.**

Avoid verbosity. Be precise. Surround yourself with
people of robust common sense.

Everybody makes mistakes. Everyone has failures.
Try to learn from them. Treat them as opportunities
to begin again more intelligently.

Practise austerity even in times of prosperity.

NARESH GOYAL

Founder-chairman of Jet Airways, Naresh Goyal has over four decades of experience in the aviation industry. His Jet Airways is the second largest airline in India in terms of market share and number of passengers. He was on the prestigious International Air Transport Association (IATA) Board of Governors from 2009-10, and again from 2011-13. He was presented the first NDTV Profit Business Award in 2006 and received a Lifetime Achievement Award by the Travel Agents Association of India in 2010. In 2011, he was conferred Belgium's Commandeur of the Order of Leopold II, one of the highest titles in the country.

SKY ISN'T THE LIMIT

At the age of twelve Naresh Goyal lost everything, except his conviction. He then went on to build one of India's best-known airlines, Jet Airways.

Naresh Goyal was born into a prosperous family of jewellers in Sangrur, Punjab. But a financial crisis destroyed everything they had. The house was auctioned and their few belongings were thrown onto the streets. Naresh was all of twelve years then. There was no money to eat or pay his school fees. They didn't even have a place to stay.

The Goyal family took refuge at Naresh's grand-uncle's home. But it wasn't as if life became much better there. The family's financial struggle continued. Naresh spent several nights studying under the streetlamps. He always believed that education was the first stepping stone to success, so even though he did not have the money to study his desired subjects of law and chartered accountancy, he made it a point to complete his graduation in commerce. 'Nothing is impossible—believe in this and drive towards realizing the truth of this, if honesty and purpose are behind it,' he says.

Nobody ever thought that this boy who had lost everything would one day build Jet Airways, one of India's leading airlines.

Naresh's story is no less than that of Chris Gardner, on whom the movie *The Pursuit of Happyness* (2006) is based. Gardner was an on-and-off salesman who, after being homeless and jobless, finally built a multi-million-dollar brokerage firm. What Naresh achieved with the little he had is inspiring. It is based on lots of hard work, luck and innovative thinking.

Taking Off

Stories of Naresh's struggle have become motivational tales for Jet Airways' employees. After finishing his graduation in 1967 at the age of eighteen, Naresh joined his great-uncle's travel agency, East West Agencies, as a cashier, at a meagre salary of ₹300 per month. The agency catered to Lebanese International Airlines. For three years, he slept in the office, often on the floor. From there he found a job as public relations manager of Lebanese Airlines. Here he hit instant success with his hard work, and worked with many international airlines like Royal Jordanian and Philippine Airlines.

When Naresh was barely twenty-five, he borrowed money from his mother to start his own agency, Jetair (Private) Limited, in 1974, which catered to international airlines for sales and distribution. Air services remained nationalized from 1953 to 1991. Only Air India and Indian Airlines were allowed to fly then. But after the opening up of the Indian economy, like many businesses, the airlines industry also got deregulated and private airlines were allowed to operate. Naresh grabbed this opportunity and set up Jet Airways in 1991. It was just the beginning.

He leased four planes from Gulf Air and Kuwait Airways and started operations on 5 May 1993. The idea behind this was that a lot of Indians who worked in the Gulf countries came from smaller cities. Goyal wanted to connect smaller cities, which he thought was a business opportunity, as most of the other flights catered more to the metros. Two of his aircrafts were received by J.R.D. Tata, often regarded as the father of Indian aviation, on arrival. He told Naresh, 'Naresh, if you cannot make Jet Airways better than the best, then send these two aircraft back today.'[1]

Remembering the incident, Naresh says, 'Be a receptive, focused, intense listener. Listen to your employees, your customers and your competitors.' And his success shows that he did listen carefully to J.R.D's advice.

However, while private airlines were allowed to fly, they were not allowed to print timetables of their flights. Since Naresh could not publish timetables, he came up with an innovative idea to publicize his flights' timings indirectly, by announcing that there was a breakfast flight (at 7.00 a.m.), a late breakfast flight (at 9.25 a.m.), a lunchtime flight (at 1.50 p.m.) and so on. This went on for a year, until the government allowed private airlines to publish their flight schedules.

---

[1] Rohit Saran and Puja Mehra, 'The King of Air', *India Today*, 6 February 2006.

Naresh also believes in leading by example. In the early days of Jet, everyone had to engage in the most mundane of tasks; even pilots had to clean toilets. On some occasions, Naresh himself cleaned the toilet to show his employees how it should be done.

Jet, Set, Go

Naresh wanted Jet Airways to be a world-class airline, which would not limit its operations to India. International routes from India were liberalized in 2004, and Jet started its first flight to London in 2005, moving later to cities like Brussels and San Francisco. The service was impeccable. The uniforms for the flight attendants were created by fashion designers, there were three-course meals in all classes, and champagne was served to the first-class flyers.

He wanted Jet to learn from the world's best—the technical efficiency of Lufthansa, the on-time performance of Swiss Air, Singapore Airlines's service quality and Qantas's accident-free record—and set these as the benchmarks for his own airline. To achieve this, he decided to get the best workforce from around the world, comprising mostly expats, like Victoriano P. Dungca, former executive vice-president of Philippine Airlines, and Ali Ghandour, the former chairman of Royal Jordanian. At one point, Jet's workforce had about 40 per cent foreigners. The top leadership jobs were always given to expats. At the time, it worked for him. For instance, Jet's second CEO, Nikos Kardassis, boosted dollar bookings[2] and increased Jet's

---

[2]Booking of tickets in India by travellers abroad.

connectivity. Eventually, Jet's dollar booking rate became higher than that of Indian Airlines. Soon enough, Jet also became the preferred airline for business flyers, and started a frequent-flyer programme.

In July 2007, in an article where he was compared to Richard Branson of Virgin, Naresh said, 'Hospitality is in our blood—to look after our guests. With us, you get a hot meal within a half-hour of takeoff. It's a three-course meal in every section of the airplane—even in coach.'[3]

Back to the Roots

In 2006, Jet was not only India's best-run airline, but one of the world's most profitable ones as well. 2006 was also the year when Naresh took the audacious decision to acquire Subrata Roy Sahara's low-cost carrier Air Sahara. The acquisition cost was ₹2,250 crore. It added twenty-seven aircrafts to Jet's fleet of fifty-three, and took the combined entity's market share to 48 per cent.

After buying Air Sahara, Naresh rebranded it as JetLite, making it a no-frills airline. In 2009, Naresh launched what was called the JetKonnect Service, which was created to manage Jet's domestic operations. From 25 March 2012, JetLite was brought under the JetKonnect umbrella. It covers 60 per cent of Jet's domestic service.

---

[3]'How Naresh Goyal Built Jet Airways', *Rediff,* http://www.rediff.com/money/2007/jul/24forbes.htm, accessed on 5 January 2015.

Though the thought was good, JetKonnect failed to connect with flyers. It did not score either in popularity or profit. Naresh finally decided to shut down JetKonnect's operations in 2014. JetLite will, however, continue to be a part of Jet Airways. Experts say that too many brands under the Jet umbrella has created confusion and further lowered the group's profits. Now IndiGo has overtaken Jet in terms of market share.

Naresh is quick at reworking things. 'Thoughts and words must be translated swiftly into correct, constructive action—time is too precious to waste away on thoughts and words only,' he says. He announced that his airline will restructure and streamline its domestic business, and create a strong master brand, Jet Airways, like it used to be when Naresh rose so far as to be called the 'Ambani' of Indian aviation.

'Connect with people at every level at all times. People up and down the line can contribute to success—listen to them, challenge them, give them opportunities, filter their talk, but always stay connected with them,' Naresh says.

Again, like the Ambanis, Naresh knows how to get out of tough situations. The aviation industry has been on the slide for a few years now. Jet, too, has been at the losing end. Losses are mounting and so is the debt. Tweaking operations wasn't enough. Naresh needed an investor. In 2013, he signed a deal with the Abu Dhabi-based Etihad Group, which also has an airline business, started in 2003, and therefore much younger than Jet. Etihad bought 24 per cent of Jet at $379 million, or ₹2,060 crore, reducing Naresh's share from 80 per cent to 51 per cent. This way, he managed to raise $600 million. The money was to be used to meet losses and pay off debts.

This is not the first time that Naresh Goyal has faced a tough situation. The takeover of Sahara was not an easy task, and almost resulted in a feud. There was also an employee problem in 2008, when the entire Jet staff decided to go on a strike after a few hundred air hostesses were laid off. Naresh came out unscathed from all these situations. 'Trust in the innate goodness of all, but be wise, discerning and on guard at all times as [their] motives may differ from your goal,' he believes.

Jet's share price has fallen by two-thirds from its peak, but Naresh is targeting a turnaround. He has a rather simple philosophy—go the whole hog. 'Be goal- and result-oriented. All action must be as arrows, aimed at a chosen target, and focused.'

NARESH GOYAL'S MANTRAS FOR SUCCESS

Nothing is impossible—believe in this and drive towards realizing the truth of this, if honesty and purpose are behind it.

Be a receptive, focused, intense listener. Listen to your employees, your customers and your competitors.

Thoughts and words must be translated swiftly into correct, constructive action—time is too precious to waste away on thoughts and words only.

Connect with people at every level at all times. People up and down the line can contribute to success—listen to them, challenge them, give them opportunities, filter their talk, but always stay connected with them.

Trust in the innate goodness of all, but be wise, discerning and on guard at all times as [their] motives may differ from your goal.

Be goal- and result-oriented. All action must be as arrows, aimed at a chosen target, and focused.

KUNAL BAHL

Kunal Bahl, a Wharton Business School graduate, is the co-founder and chief executive officer of Snapdeal, India's largest online marketplace. Launched as recently as February 2010, Snapdeal now has a network of more than 60,000 brands and merchants, and caters to 40 million members across 4,000 towns and cities. It has 5 million products across 500 diverse categories.

THE ONLINE MAVERICK

Kunal Bahl has taken many risks and changed course several times to make Snapdeal India's largest e-commerce marketplace.

In May 2014, the entire ceiling at Snapdeal's office in Delhi was covered in red danglers that said 'Mission 500'. Ask Kunal Bahl, co-founder and CEO of the e-commerce company, what the mission is, and he laughs. 'That's internal goal setting,' he says, but won't disclose what the goal is. That is how his company is run—the year is broken into four quarters and every quarter has a goal.

Kunal, who founded the company with his friend Rohit Bansal (not related to the Bansals of Flipkart, a Snapdeal rival), believes in doing everything at high speed and achieving scale. In the e-commerce business, he says, it is nearly impossible to run without these two attributes. Snapdeal has a revenue run rate of more than a billion dollars (i.e. an average monthly sale of ₹500 crore) and is already the country's largest e-commerce marketplace, an online business model where other merchants can put up their stuff on the site for sale.

Be it fund-raising, adding sellers to its platform, or adding a growing number of items on its site, Snapdeal ranks as one of the top three e-commerce companies in India. The e-commerce business in India is all about the number of sellers, as well as providing huge discounts and big valuations, and Snapdeal has been at the forefront. And the credit for this goes to the face and co-founder of the company—Kunal Bahl.

One of the things that he and the top leadership does is set goals, which he likes to call 'BHAGs' (Big Hairy Audacious Goals). The term, which means 'run' in Hindi, was first used by Jim Collins and Jerry I. Porras in their seminal work *Built to Last*. It denotes a goal that should be unachievable. And how does he measure that? His says that once people in the office get to know of the BHAG, they should either jump off their seats out of anxiety or say that attaining it would be near-impossible. If Kunal gets either of these reactions, he knows that he has set the bar high enough.

Is Kunal a sadist who loves to torture his employees? That is not the case; he just thinks that if the goals are set pretty high, people push themselves to try new things, which helps them reach the goals faster. He often calls Snapdeal a missionary company, where each member of the team is out there to achieve a larger objective. 'If you want happiness for a lifetime, you need a larger purpose,' he says. 'Our purpose is to create life-changing experiences for about 1 million businesses through technology.'

Once the supply that comes from the merchants is in place,

the bigger challenge is to create demand. And it is important to maintain the balance, for if either one slows down or moves faster than the other, it might create too many customers with too little to offer to them, or vice-versa. Making the entire workforce focus on achieving the goal is another challenge; after all, mobilizing more than 2,000 people isn't easy.

After the mission is decided, the team goes into a ten-day planning period. Right after that, a review of the previous quarter is done. Employees, in groups and individually, talk about their contributions. In an interview, Kunal said, 'If you don't stitch a company together really, really well, it falls apart really quickly. And this is almost like an adhesive that keeps everything together.'

There have been more than seven quarters of goal-setting now—the first one was Mission 30 in late 2012. Snapdeal's monthly revenue then was not more than ₹7 crore then. In one quarter, Kunal and Rohit decided that the revenue should be ₹30 crore every month. In another, they focused on Mission NPS, or improvement in the net promoter score—a parameter which determines the quality of user experience on the site. The score for most e-commerce companies' NPS was anywhere between thirty-five and fifty. Kunal wanted it at sixty-five for Snapdeal. Both these goals were achieved. Then they set a goal called Mission 24, where Kunal vouched that 75 per cent of their orders would be shipped within twenty-four hours. By the end of that quarter, Snapdeal was shipping 80 per cent of its orders within the allotted time frame.

Many businesses in the e-commerce industry, which were

flourishing before Snapdeal was started, have either perished or been reduced to nothing today, like Naaptol, Tradus and Yebhi. Snapdeal, meanwhile, is now India's largest marketplace with more than 60,000 sellers. Kunal really knows his business well. In the beginning, though, the journey was rocky.

Offline to Online

Kunal and Rohit studied together in school. Both sat for the IIT-JEE, but only Rohit got through. Kunal went on to get a degree from Wharton Business School. After his graduation, he got a job with Microsoft in the US. He applied for a work visa, but that got rejected and he was deported back to India. This was a big setback, because Kunal had been the first person in his family to go to the US. So he settled for working with a mechanical engineering firm, which made plastic moulds.

Kunal was also a research assistant and has taken courses in writing, the history of Jewish art, Western classical music and ethnic conflict around the world. He is particularly interested in cults.

In 2007, Kunal thought of starting his own business. At the time, Rohit Bansal was working with Capital One, a financing company, and was being sent to the US. Kunal called him and asked him to stay back. Rohit agreed, and they started a business of discount coupons together, called Money Saver, in 2007. That was a big decision for Rohit, given that he was from a very small town called Malot in Punjab, where people do not usually get opportunities to go abroad.

The first office for Money Saver was in a basement in the Kirti Nagar furniture market of New Delhi. Kunal and Rohit scoured the streets of Delhi to tie up with spas, restaurants and such businesses. Most of the businesses did not even know what coupons were. Kunal and Rohit were both young, so to look older they wore coats even in the 45-degree Delhi heat. Kunal remembers how Rohit once waited outside the office of an international shoe brand for seven hours.

Both Kunal and Rohit had a calling sheet and would call a merchant every two days. If they did not respond in three attempts, they would visit the stores. They refer to this as 'standing ovation', since they would actually stand in front of the merchant's office until the merchant agreed to meet them. Eventually they managed to sign up all the big brands—United Colours of Benetton, Adidas, Levi's, the works.

Kunal and Rohit initially believed that their business would one day earn billions in revenue, but that was not to be. They only sold 20,000 coupons. But it worked out well eventually, as most of the brands from that time are still with them.

But at the time, things were not easy. At one point the situation was such that there was only ₹21,000 left in their bank account, after paying salaries. They had two options—to close down and exit, or put in all they had and continue to run the business. They chose the latter, albeit in a new avatar—the online deals business.

When Snapdeal was launched in 2010, it was the seventh such company. Within six months, there were fifty other sites. However, in fourteen months, Snapdeal cornered a 70 per cent market share in this space (American deals company Groupon had not then entered India). They had also raised $10 million. But a China trip was to change everything.

A New Snapdeal

In 2011, Kunal and Rohit travelled to China. There, they came across Alibaba, a home-grown e-commerce marketplace. It seemed that everyone in China was a retailer with Alibaba. That's when Kunal realized how product e-commerce in India could take off. At that time, in India, there was no real online marketplace except eBay. That's when they decided to build a product marketplace, as compared to the inventory-based business model of most e-commerce companies. They also decided to focus on the 93 per cent unorganized market.

E-commerce is a dynamic industry, says Kunal. One needs to keep changing. 'It is important to be intellectually honest, and the only way to do it is to tell yourself [that] if you don't do it, you will die.'

By then, Snapdeal had raised another $57 million. 'There were [some] key turning points in our business. There were many pivots. Earlier it was easy, but as the business got larger, the expectations of the venture capitalists [and] shareholders changed,' says Kunal. 'The deals business would not be large enough to justify the capital raised.'

After returning to India in December 2011, Kunal told his board of directors that he wanted to pivot the entire company to a marketplace model. The deals business was making a decent amount of money, but Kunal decided to shut it down. 'We could have hired someone [new] and then tried to figure it out, but we knew that the marketplace business was going to be a bigger business,' says Kunal. 'We shifted the best people from the deals business to the marketplace business.'

The partners started expanding the business aggressively. Today, Snapdeal has more than 25 million visitors and earns a billion dollars in revenue annually. 'Our aspiration is to have certainty of availability of products, at the best prices,' says Kunal.

Getting in Ratan Tata

By 2013, Snapdeal was growing at 600 per cent, and fundraising was getting easier. It was then that the company caught the eye of the former head of the Tata group, Ratan Tata. Ratan Tata wanted to meet with the founders, and they met at Bombay House, the Tata headquarters. At the meeting, the Tata honcho asked Kunal what the 'purpose' of Snapdeal was. 'He was fascinated by [Snapdeal's] growth,' says Kunal. 'He said, if you would have come and said this [600 per cent growth] a few years ago, I would not have believed you.'

The meeting went on for one hour and by the end of it Ratan Tata made up his mind to invest in the company. 'But the more important part was the validation that he has partnered with us,' feels Kunal.

Kunal believes that Ratan Tata's expertise will help Snapdeal understand how to build business to scale, and face the challenges that organizations face. He will help Snapdeal grow into a truly great company in the next twenty-five years.

The seed capital was great. In February 2013, eBay bought a stake in Snapdeal, which helped the company start two new service lines. Snapdeal thereafter launched a logistics platform, Safeship, which integrated several courier companies on a single platform. This helped in tie-ups with the sellers, as now the most efficient courier company could be picked out of several, depending on the place of delivery, to fulfil the orders. Safeship was pioneered by eBay under the name Powership.

The other service was TrustPay, similar to eBay's PaisaPay. It was started by Snapdeal in April 2013. Through this, once the product is purchased, the money is not immediately dispatched to the seller. Instead, it sits in an escrow account for seven days. If there's any failure in delivery of the product, the money is returned to the buyer. eBay and Snapdeal also help each other by cross-selling products.

Miles to Go

Kunal has had a successful run so far. Snapdeal is now venturing into mobile commerce, like most of its rivals, with the launch of its mobile phone app. Kunal says this is another pivot in the company's life—it went from offline to online; from deals to products; and now, from computers to mobiles.

Makes sense, since India has more than 200 million Internet connections, out of which 150 million are through smartphones. A new team was created for the mobile app, and was urged to compete with the PC team. About 55 to 65 per cent of

Snapdeal's orders come on mobile, at present; Kunal expects that to rise to 80 per cent in the next couple of years. The company is already ready for that transition. The conversion in transaction[1], Kunal says, is also 20 per cent higher on mobiles than on PCs.

In 2014, when Flipkart, India's largest e-commerce site, was valued at $7 billion, many experts thought that the Indian e-commerce industry was heading into a bubble, which would soon burst. But soon enough it was clear that raising capital was the rule of the game, and anyone who could not do so would not be able to remain in the business. Kunal understood that very well. In October 2014, Snapdeal raised $627 million from Softbank, which is also an investor in Alibaba, the world's largest e-commerce website by value, and Snapdeal's inspiration.

Even though Kunal is on his way to becoming an e-billionaire today, some old habits die hard. Kunal had to bootstrap the company in the beginning and there was no place for wastages. Even now, everyone in Snapdeal travels economy class, including Kunal. He still drives a second-hand Honda Civic.

With the team he has, no obstacle is impossible to overcome. Kunal and Rohit have, in over five years, created an organization so hungry for growth and so aggressive to win that it has turned into a mean machine out to conquer the world of electronic retailing. Kunal jokes, 'If our team puts their heads together, we can even launch a rocket.' Knowing him, that might just be the next goal.

---

[1] Actual buyers as opposed to only site visitors.

KUNAL BAHL'S MANTRAS FOR SUCCESS

If you want happiness for a lifetime, you need a larger purpose. Our purpose is to create life-changing experiences for about one million businesses through technology.

If you don't stitch a company together really, really well, it falls apart really quickly.

It is important to be intellectually honest, and the only way to do it is to tell yourself [that] if you don't do it, you will die.

If the goals are set pretty high, people push themselves to try new things, which helps them reach their goals faster. If our team puts their heads together, we can even launch a rocket.

RAHUL SHARMA

Co-founder and chief executive officer of Micromax Informatics Limited, Rahul Sharma is largely responsible for Micromax's unprecedented success, making it the tenth largest mobile phone company in the world. With more than sixty mobile phone models ranging across the spectrum, Micromax Informatics Limited became a billion-dollar company in 2013-14. Rahul Sharma was named among Forbes' Persons of the Year in 2010 and received an award for Excellence in Business at the *GQ* Men of the Year awards in 2013.

MAXIMIZING SUCCESS

Rahul Sharma loves cars, and Micromax. In less than a decade, he has made Micromax one of India's largest handset manufacturers, one that is giving multinationals a run for their money.

In 2014, Rahul Sharma, one of the four founders of Micromax, went to Harvard Business School to do a short management course. One day, the professor at one of his classes was discussing a case study on Apple. Rahul doesn't want to name the professor, but says that he had worked with Steve Jobs for a long time, since the beginning of Apple, and was on the board of many large multinationals. The professor knew Apple through and through, and felt that the company was not moving on the right path. He asked everyone, including Rahul, what piece of advice they would give to Tim Cook, the current CEO of Apple, if they met him on a plane for five minutes.

Everyone in the room had an answer to the professor's question. Rahul's was different from them all. Recalling that incident, Rahul says with a smile, 'I didn't give any advice. *Tum ₹60,000 ka phone bechte raho* [you keep selling phones for ₹60,000], and we will be very happy.'

Why not?

Apple targets premium smartphone buyers, a market where Micromax doesn't compete. Rahul is happy not to have Apple as its competitor, as he already has to deal with the likes of Samsung, HTC, Motorola and many others. Micromax is the largest Indian mobile manufacturer and Rahul is the face of the brand, whom the world credits for the meteoric rise of the low-cost Indian handset. According to him, 'It is all about how you understand consumers and solve their problems. Identify the complex problems and solve them, I think that's the mantra.'

Rahul came out with QWERTY phones in 2009. Back then, Micromax sold 125,000 phones every month. But that was not the only product which came out of Micromax's stable. Based on consumer trends, Rahul's team figured out that recharging phones was a big problem in rural India due to the lack of electricity. So Micromax brought out the X1i, with a battery life of up to thirty days, at an affordable price of ₹2,150. It made up 85 per cent of Micromax's sales in 2008-09. In 2010, it came out with the Bling series—Swarovski-encrusted phones aimed at women.

At the time, the Indian telecom industry was booming— telephone tariffs were going down, and there were multiple talk-time schemes for different kinds of usage. People were taking multiple connections—often using one for local calls and another for outstation or international calls. Micromax phones with dual SIM capability became an instant hit with such consumers. Next up was a phone in partnership with MTV, which had Yamaha speakers, meant for playing loud music. In the pipeline was also a Windows Mobile operating system (OS)-based phone. The Android OS was still nascent then, but Rahul was already talking to Google for Android-based phones, in an attempt to play in the higher end of the smartphone market. He also came up with an innovative multitasking phone for the rural market, which doubled up as a mosquito repellent, and another one for an urban target audience, which could function as an alternate remote control for one's television and air-conditioner!

But there was one thing every phone Micromax launched had in common—each one was affordable and meant for the masses. Along with the rise of Micromax, India saw new home-grown as well as foreign mobile brands being launched every week, sometimes every second day. At one point there were more than 160 home-grown brands in India, all importing handsets made in China and Taiwan, all of them after the same set of customers. Rahul had to differentiate his company somehow.

A Giant Leap

Rahul had learnt the ropes of marketing even before he started selling mobiles. Micromax was not always a mobile handset maker. It was started in 1991 by Rajesh Agarwal as Micromax Informatics Limited for distribution of computer hardware. In 1999, Rahul, Sumeet Kumar and Vikas Jain joined as equal partners. Apart from selling computers and offering software courses, the company also sold fixed wireless phone instruments for Public Call Offices (PCOs) owned by Airtel. A million of these PCOs were still operational at the time. It was in 2008 that Rahul came up with the idea of entering the mobile phone segment and convinced the other partners to go along as well.

Smartphones were then slowly becoming the 'in' thing for the hip and the urbane. Samsung had launched its new series of Galaxy smartphones, with an Android OS, in 2009. Soon, Micromax, too, had launched its own version of Android phones, the Canvas series. In cities, people were abandoning famous brands in favour of the Canvas phones. The second-generation Canvas was launched exclusively on Flipkart, and the website soon ran out of stock. Some customers were even willing to pay a premium for the phone. Later, when it was available elsewhere as well, it did phenomenally well. In January 2012 alone, the phone sold 174,000 units.

One of the reasons for this success was the strikingly successful brand campaigns by Micromax. It had Akshay Kumar as its brand ambassador in India since 2010, and later it hired Hollywood star Hugh Jackman too. Its tagline—'Nothing like Anything'—was also an instant hit.

A lot of this is due to Rahul's marketing prowess. He wasn't born rich. His father was a school principal, and he grew up in Teacher's Colony in Delhi. Even as a college student, when most of his friends would pick up a *Gladrags* or any other fashion magazine from the neighbourhood book stalls, Rahul would pick up an *A&M*, short for *Advertising and Marketing*,

India's leading magazine on the titular subjects, which got discontinued later. 'Since my schooldays I have been more intrigued by marketing. I used to have all the *A&Ms*,' he says.

In college, he still remembers that the difference between the meanings of sales and marketing was a bit skewed. Students memorized the definition of both the terms without really understanding it. 'Once you start implementing both, you understand the difference,' smiles Rahul.

Cut to 2012. Micromax was heading the domestic pack, with others like Karbonn, Lava and Intex following closely behind. Rahul soon realized that importing only from China was not a sustainable business model. To stay in the business and separate Micromax from the rest, he decided to streamline the company's operations and entered into tie-ups with chipset makers Qualcomm and MediaTek. Rahul also created a plan through which he could keep a closer watch on the distribution. His team tracked retail sales on a daily basis and saw to it that there was no inventory pile-up with any of the retailers or distributors. He also established a design and research centre, and had a team that consulted with third-party manufacturers in China.

All this would not have been possible without his passion for the business. 'You have to be very driven…passionate about what you are doing,' he says. 'Passion is fundamental, and passion can be in anything—it can be in photography, or in writing. You just need to follow that.'

The other thing that is important to be successful, according to Rahul, is to understand one's 'DNA' (by which he means one's aptitude). 'If you have the DNA for finance, you can't do marketing. If you have the DNA that lies more in building material, and you want to do something online... [that does not work].'

Micromax has already gone through the rigour. It took a year off from its fast-paced growth. Revenues fell and profits declined—all for restructuring the company for the future. It was a well-calculated bet—in the next two years, revenue went up five times and profits twenty times. This was also the time when Rahul hired a professional CEO, a head for feature phones and one for smartphones.

Rahul holds short of 20 per cent stake in Micromax. The company's progress is reflected in his lifestyle. The bachelor owns a Merc and a BMW, apart from a limited-edition orange Bentley, and lives in a farmhouse, spread over 3 acres of property in Delhi. In the last two years, Rahul has also become one of the country's highest tax payers.

Beyond Indian Shores

Once Rahul had established the brand in India, it was time to go overseas. However, this strategy had not worked for Micromaxs earlier. An attempt to go to Nigeria and Brazil in 2010 failed. Micromax was and still is selling in the United Arab Emirates in a small way, though, and in West Asia through retail chains like Carrefour. But in 2010 it was felt that Micromax was spreading itself too thin. So Rahul and the other founders decided to regroup and concentrate on the Indian subcontinent—it is now present in Sri Lanka, Nepal and Bangladesh apart from India, and in all these places it is one of the top three handset makers.

In 2013, Rahul again started charting out the company's international roadmap. The first country where Micromax was launched internationally this time was Russia, in January 2014. When Micromax entered Russia, Rahul faced a different kind of challenge. Unlike India, where smartphones comprised 19 per cent of the market, Russia had a smartphone base of 40 per cent, and some well-established brands. Even though it was a challenge to break through this, Rahul had tackled a similar situation in India, early in Micromax's life. It's still early days, but Rahul knows how to disrupt the hierarchy using smart, innovative products and marketing.

Rahul believes Russia will serve as a gateway for Micromax to enter Eastern Europe. Eastern Europe, unlike the US, is not a bundled market (where phones come under contract with mobile connections and with lock-in periods) but a retail market, like in India, which he is familiar with. The next country in line is Romania, and thereafter he plans to take his company to Czech Republic, Poland and Slovakia. Rahul believes that if the brand is successful in Russia, it will not be very difficult to get into the other countries. Unlike the last time Micromax tried going international, now it has more financial muscle to penetrate into these countries and that is what Rahul is doing, although now more cautiously.

Seven years ago, in 2007-08, Micromax was making just ₹16 crore by selling fixed wireless handsets. All that Rahul could aspire for was to reach ₹1,000 crore in the next few years. By

2013-14, the company had grown 500 times and clocked a revenue of ₹7,500 crore. According to some industry insiders, in 2014-15, Micromax will cross ₹10,000 crore in revenue. International markets will play an important role hereon.

The Road Ahead

Rahul says that there is no debt on Micromax's balance sheet, and he does not need money to go for any expansion plan. Ask him if he wants to do an initial public offer (IPO), or raise capital from a private equity firm and he says, 'We don't think we need equity infusion from outside. The company is growing at the right pace. But whenever we feel that we need equity, we will go out and raise that money.'

He has been busy, but that alone is not enough. 'It is important to have something new in life always,' he feels. He has launched another new mobile phone brand, YU, which is a Micromax subsidiary but will be run by a completely different team and will have a new CEO. Rahul says that this will be a game changer.

The new handsets will be based on the Cyanogen platform, and Micromax has signed an exclusive contract with the Silicon Valley-based firm. The focus of the device will be on services, like health, education and so on, not through apps but directly. The handset will only be an enabler. This will also take Rahul back to his roots, when he had tried his hand at software products.

If YU succeeds Sharma will have his hands full. He has taken time off from Micromax to concentrate on this new venture.

There is one thing that he says is common across all his employees: 'We all work and live for Micromax.' The main target which he wants to achieve one day is to have Micromax counted among the world's topmost companies. 'If you see an Indian company in the list of the top five globally, it's a big thing.'

RAHUL SHARMA'S MANTRAS FOR SUCCESS

It is all about how you understand consumers and solve their problems. Identify the complex problems and solve them.

You have to be very driven...passionate about what you are doing. Passion is fundamental.

If you have the DNA [aptitude] for finance, you can't do marketing. If you have the DNA that lies more in building material, and you want to do something online... [that does not work].

Disrupt the hierarchy using smart, innovative products and marketing.

It is important to have something new in life always.

RAJIV MEMANI

Rajiv Memani has been associated with Ernst & Young (EY) for almost twenty years, and took over as the chairman of EY India in 2005. He is also part of the Global Executive Board of EY as the chairman of the Emerging Markets Committee. EY is India's largest, and the world's third-largest, professional services firm. Rajiv Memani is also the chairman of the Accounting Standard Committee, Confederation of Indian Industry (CII). He is a part of the World Economic Forum's New Asian Leaders, a network of 100 young leaders in business and politics, to develop programmes for Asia's development.

THE DISCIPLE

Rajiv Memani is deeply inspired by the teachings of Swami Vivekananda, which he believes have helped him lead Ernst & Young (EY) and make it one of India's leading consultancy firms.

A huge portrait of Swami Vivekananda hangs in the lobby of the EY office in Gurgaon. There are also many more small- and medium-sized frames of the Swami's teachings all over the office. One of the sayings goes:

Take up one idea. Make that one idea your life—think of it, dream of it, live on that idea. Let the brain, muscles, nerves, every part of your body, be full of that idea, and just leave every other idea alone. This is the way to success.

'He [Vivekananda] believed in service and strong character. Ramakrishna Missions around the world have institutionalized these qualities really well. He was also the first person who believed in a strong and powerful India,' says Rajiv Memani, chairman of EY India, India's largest consultancy house.

The Ace Accountant

Rajiv was born in Calcutta. His father Kashi Nath Memani was the country managing partner of S.R. Batliboi & Company, an accounting firm founded in 1914 in Calcutta. In 1970, the Naxalite movement in Calcutta forced the Memanis to shift to Delhi, and provided Kashi Nath the opportunity to expand the company's operations to Delhi. The Calcutta house of the Memanis still exists and Rajiv visits the city whenever he can.

After moving to Delhi, Rajiv finished his schooling from Delhi Public School, RK Puram, and completed his graduation in commerce from Shri Ram College of Commerce (SRCC). In those days, he would attend college in the morning and go to Batliboi in the evening to do his articleship. That's where he got his grooming as an accountant, and later completed his chartered accountancy in 1991.

The Batliboi firm has an interesting history of forging global partnerships. In 1950, it became a member-firm of Arthur Young & Company, the nineteenth-century accountancy firm. Arthur Young merged with Ernst & Whinney in 1989 to form EY. At the time, there were two firms representing EY in India—S.R. Batliboi & Co. and S.B. Billimoria & Co. In 1995, EY decided to start its India operations and Kashi Nath was appointed the head of EY India. They also chose S.R. Batliboi & Co. as their sole representative member-firm in India.

This was also the time when the days of the licence raj came to an end. Multinationals started entering India in hordes. This was radically different from earlier, when international companies like Gillette and Xerox would only get into small joint ventures in India. It was a new beginning for India.

'When the new companies came, a lot of things changed. There was a lot of competition. In the professional services firms (like in EY) a lot changed,' says Rajiv. He, and others like him working in the field of professional consultancy and advice, had to relearn everything from scratch. 'The change was so fast that it didn't matter how long you had worked. Everything was new. The entire consulting landscape changed, investment banking changed. Due diligence had come in. Earlier, acquisitions were on book value,' he explains.

That period, Rajiv says, was when he learnt the most. There were no PowerPoint presentations; Rajiv did long conference calls with people around the world and told them about the changes happening in India.

Rajiv knows that it is important to let go and empower others, something he learnt at an early age from his father. He remembers how, when he was only twenty-six, his father had engaged him in a valuation project of one of India's largest manufacturing groups. People on the other side were in their fifties. Rajiv had held his own and was successful in putting across his firm's point of view to the client.

Soon enough, Rajiv made his mark. 'I was the seventh partner in EY India [in 1996],' he recalls. (At present, the company has close to 270 partners in India, the highest in the industry.)

He also learnt the importance of relationships and how it was sometimes necessary to say 'no' to clients, even if it meant losing a deal. 'You say no because you don't think it will make value for the client. Or suggest someone who is better at it,' says Rajiv. When clients are not credible, he has often walked away from negotiations. 'From the institutional standpoint, it builds a company culture, based on very strong ethics and principles. From a client standpoint, you build a deep and enduring relationship with your business partners.'

Sometimes, he says, taking these decisions becomes a 'moral dilemma on a weekly basis'. But then, an accountant has to live on credibility. 'When you are working up the ladder, your key attribute is your credibility. If you have to build creditable relationships with clients, you need do the right things.'

Over the years, he has also told his clients to take decisions that may not seem attractive in the short term but will pay rich dividends over a long period. Once, he advised a cement company not to sell its assets to tide over a difficult period. A few years later, the company became Rajasthan's largest cement manufacturer. In another instance, in 2003, a large construction company had almost signed a joint venture with a foreign company. Rajiv asked the promoters not to go ahead with the deal. As things turned out, over the next five to six years, India had the highest growth rate in real estate and the construction company grew by leaps and bounds. However, there have been some instances when clients haven't listened to him, gone ahead with their decisions and repented later.

It's not as if EY got it right every time. There have been failures occasionally. For Rajiv, it is important to build client relationships that can survive the difficult times. And the only way to do that is by building credibility.

Leading from the Front

Rajiv takes mistakes very seriously. 'We spend more time analysing failures,' he says. 'We are always paranoid about what went wrong. We don't spend a lot of our time celebrating our wins. But we do not blame a person for the failure.' One of the most important things for him is to learn from failures, but at the same time to let go and carry on. 'There are issues in every project and it is important to learn from them.'

He often sees his colleagues unhappy with the progress of their projects. One way of making projects successful is teamwork. 'Never be shy of taking help from other team members who might know more than you. The other thing is to learn from the problems one faces in every project, and the third is to look ahead—how do you improve and how to rectify your mistakes, in order to ensure you never repeat them? Lastly, just in case things do not go as planned, always have a contingency plan,' he says.

A way to build this teamwork is through an internal mentorship programme. EY has some such programmes but Rajiv admits that there is scope to do a lot more in terms of mentoring young associates.

This is the new EY, under Rajiv, very different from how it was in 1996 when he first became a partner. Then the firm had only 200 people.

Rajiv soon rose to become EY's national director of corporate finance and set up the practice in India all by himself. In 1997, EY, which was then the world's second-largest management consultancy firm, decided to invest $2 billion in India. It approached the Foreign Investment Promotion Board (FIPB). David Shpilberg, vice chairman of EY, Asia Pacific, told *Business Standard* at the time: 'We believe India has globalized. In the next five to ten years, Indian business and services will integrate with the rest of the world and we want to be a part of it.'[1]

In 2002, EY bought Arthur Andersen's (a Chicago-based multinational accounting firm) operations in India and several other countries. Rajiv became the CEO and the country managing partner of EY India in 2004. A year later, he was appointed chairman.

In the subsequent years the business grew, but no one knew what was coming. In 2008, the global recession hit everyone, and EY was no exception. 'Leadership during downturn is critical,' Rajiv says, remembering those times.

Once again after 1991, the business model changed overnight. Rajiv had to cut costs and run a lean organization, but more importantly, he had to reduce EY's risk exposure. The company stopped exploring new revenue streams and discontinued investing in projects he calls 'experiments that might bear fruit few years later'. Some very hard decisions had to be taken. 'We decided that we will only do projects that are profitable. Mindset of growth is very different when the economy is

---

[1] 'Ernst & Young in Consultancy Venture with S.R. Batliboi', *Business Standard*, 12 November 1997.

good. At times you need to take unpopular decisions, including firing people, but then that's the reflection of the [falling] economy.'

After the economy started looking up again, Rajiv decided to bring back the 'experiments'. He decided to engage more with EY's workforce and encouraged them to come up with innovative ideas. By then, Facebook had become popular. Rajiv figured out that social media was a good way to engage with people. 'I think you have to win the hearts and minds of people. You need to get people positively motivated to get the best out of them,' he says. This also helped him strengthen the EY DNA within the organization. Apart from interactions on social media, he also has town hall meetings and breakfast meetings with team members to learn more about them.

Rajiv takes huge pride in having created a cohesive partnership group with the maximum number of partners any consultancy practice in India has: 'It has given stability to the firm, and allows you to pass the ball.' Over the years, he has made EY a more entrepreneurial market-focused workplace. Partners in the group have sustained a great relationship with all its stakeholders—the government, banks and companies. His initiatives in India were so well-recognized that he was appointed to be a part of EY's global Emerging Markets Committee.

Despite Rajiv's alertness and focus, he has missed a few opportunities. But that does not bother him much. What matters to him is to ensure that EY doesn't miss any big bets and, at the same time, makes future choices that will help the company grow. Opportunities can be picked up by anyone; what matters is how they are executed. 'We could have entered the digital business two years back. We have done so now,' he states.

But every new business brings its own set of challenges. Remembering the Satyam scam, Rajiv says, 'You don't want to get into an accident like that. It's good to remain paranoid.' At the same time, 'things can and will go wrong'. What matters in the end is safeguarding the interests of the client. 'If there is an unhappy client, you need to know about it and address the issues' is his advice.

Rajiv knows that he cannot do everything on his own. He has, in his leadership team, people with expertise in areas where he himself is weak. He knows he needs to maintain the quality of work within the organization. 'There are some things you cannot let go. If there is a quality problem, if something does happen, you need to act quickly. If there is an incident like Uber [the sexual assault of a passenger by an Uber cab driver in December 2014 in Delhi], you need to act instantaneously. Our only asset is our brand. We don't have any other asset. You have to protect your assets very well.'

Most of Rajiv's time is taken up by clients, something that has not changed in many years. He feels that these clients have become a lot more demanding nowadays. They expect consultancy firms to come up with better solutions that will benefit them.

Does he have a signature leadership style?

'To be a good leader you have to be who you are. I think in a leader, fairness, equality, being objective in decision-making and being responsible is critical. That is how you can be transparent,' he advises.

To put things in perspective, he gives an example from mythology. 'If you see the Mahabharata, Yudhishthira [eldest of the five Pandavas] was the leader—above Arjuna, who was a great warrior, and Bhima, who had all the strength—because of his fairness and strong sense of judgement.'

One thing is for sure, this disciple of Vivekananda has created a legacy of his own in the world of management consultancy.

RAJIV MEMANI'S MANTRAS FOR SUCCESS

It is important to let go and empower others.

When you are working up the ladder, your key attribute is your credibility. If you have to build creditable relationships with clients, you need do the right things.

We spend more time analysing failures. We are always paranoid about what went wrong. We don't spend a lot of our time celebrating our wins. But we do not blame a person for the failure.

Never be shy of taking help from other team members who might know more than you.

Just in case things do not go as planned, always have a contingency plan.

Leadership during downturn is critical. At times you need to take unpopular decisions.

You need to get people positively motivated to get the best out of them.

If there is an unhappy client, you need to know about it and address the issues.

To be a good leader you have to be who you are. I think in a leader, fairness, equality, being objective in decision-making and being responsible is critical.

ADITYA GHOSH

Aditya Ghosh is the president, IndiGo, InterGlobe Aviation, and a member of its executive committee. He joined the board of IndiGo in May 2007 and took on the role of its president in August 2008. He has been featured in *Fortune*'s Global 40 Under 40 series for 2012 as one of the hottest young stars in business globally. He was ranked twenty-seventh in a list that includes the likes of Mark Zuckerberg of Facebook, Larry Page and Sergey Brin of Google, Marissa Mayer of Yahoo and many others. IndiGo is the world's fastest-growing low-cost carrier and India's largest airline by market share. It has won the Skytrax Award for Best Low-cost Carrier five years in a row, since 2010.

THE PERFECT TAKE-OFF

The riveting story of how Aditya Ghosh went from being a lawyer to building India's most profitable airline company while the airline industry was reeling under economic problems.

Aditya Ghosh's chhoto-mama (his mother's younger brother) once recited a poem to him—'The Road Not Taken' by Robert Frost. Aditya was then quite young, but the lines still resonate:

> *I shall be telling this with a sigh,*
> *Somewhere ages and ages hence:*
> *Two roads diverged in a wood, and I,*
> *I took the one less travelled by,*
> *And that has made all the difference.*

Aditya is not a pilot and has never studied aviation (except on the job), yet he runs the country's youngest and most profitable airline, which also has the highest market share by passengers. Formally, he graduated as a lawyer from Delhi University.

When he was still in his first year of law, he had a discussion on the legal profession with established corporate lawyer Jyoti Sagar, who was his father's friend. The discussion turned into a grilling session for Sagar. He was impressed and asked Aditya to join his firm, J. Sagar Associates, as his executive assistant.

Aditya assisted Sagar in the high-profile basmati and turmeric patent case, which the firm won. He also worked with K&S Partners, owned by Sagar, which dealt in intellectual rights and patent matters. InterGlobe Aviation Ltd, which is the holding company for IndiGo, was Sagar's client, and Aditya started handling their cases.

And, in 2004, when Aditya was just twenty-eight, he got the job of a general counsel at InterGlobe. He started working on legal matters surrounding IndiGo's launch right from the beginning—from the first order of the 100-odd aircrafts to building the team to run IndiGo. For the first few years, the business was run by aviation veteran Bruce Ashby. In 2007, the founders of IndiGo, Rahul Bhatia and Rakesh Gangwal, invited Aditya to join the board of IndiGo. Thereafter, once Bruce left in August 2008, Aditya was asked to run the company.

At the time, Aditya Ghosh was just thirty-two. The rapid turn of events surprised him, and he often calls it his 'luck'. But Rahul and Rakesh must have seen more than just a 'lucky' lawyer in him—after all, he was involved in the business planning from the very first day. 'He [Aditya] collaborated with the founders on the airline's business plan, contractual arrangements with aircraft manufacturers and engine manufacturers, recruitments, fixing contracts and allotments in airports,' reported *The Economic Times* in a 2012 article.[1] He was involved because all these components required legal intervention. For Aditya, it was his entry into the world of aviation.

Aditya wants all IndiGo aircrafts to look the same inside and outside. The packaging of the in-flight products is unique, as well as the uniforms of its staff. Aditya's perfectionism is reflected in an incident that took place during the inaugural IndiGo flight from Delhi to Guwahati. After realizing that the ladder and tractor which were to be used by passengers to disembark had reached only the night before the flight was scheduled, and were not IndiGo's signature blue colour, Aditya asked the team to paint the ladder blue overnight and run with it up and down the tarmac so that the paint dried.

IndiGo flights are notable for being punctual, a point highlighted in all their ads. Over the years, IndiGo has managed to be the most punctual of all airlines with an on-time performance of 90 per cent, something it has learnt from Singapore Airlines.

One of the success mantras Aditya believes in is giving the best of his ability. 'There is a fundamental difference between the "best of our efforts" and the "best of our ability",' he says. 'This I learnt from Mr Rakesh Gangwal. A lot of people work hard and put in their best efforts. And depending on how tired or energetic you feel that day, the extent of your effort changes. However, we realize our true potential…things that we can

---

[1] Binoy Prabhakar, 'How IndiGo's Aditya Ghosh Is the Only Airline Boss Still Flying', *The Economic Times*, 3 June 2012.

do to the best of our ability, only once in a while. Therefore it is important to strive to the "best of our ability" and not just to the "best of our efforts".'

For Aditya, IndiGo's people are its biggest assets. He interviews every new hire himself, be it pilots or airhostesses, mechanics or drivers. Once he has hired someone, he trusts the person and empowers him or her as much as he can. According to him, he is not the only one to run the 'IndiGo show'. 'Never let ego come in the way of wisdom (I feel this is particularly important for young leaders who often make the mistake of believing that they are "in charge"!).' There have been instances when he has declined to give interviews to the press because he is not comfortable talking about his laurels.

Aditya once read a story about Charles Plumb, a US Navy jet pilot in Vietnam, whose plane was destroyed by a surface-to-air missile. Charles, however, ejected and parachuted into enemy land. He was captured and spent six years in a Vietnamese prison. After his release, one day, when Charles and his wife were sitting in a restaurant, a man came up to him and told him that he had packed Charles's parachute. Charles was full of gratitude—if this man's parachute hadn't worked, he wouldn't be alive. And Aditya never forgets to thank the people who make things happen on the ground: 'We should never be shy of thinking of, and thanking, all those who pack our parachutes every day, because of whom we can be the heroes that we are and come back home alive.'

Every Penny Counts

IndiGo prides itself on being a no-frills airline. It doesn't have any frequent-flyer programmes, it has not built any exclusive airport lounges for its passengers, it doesn't offer any special check-in counters and doesn't have television screens on its flights.

Aditya wants to stay cost-efficient. Global brands which are still doing well, like Southwest Airlines, Allegiant Air, Ryanair and Spirit Airlines, focus on containing cost, year after year. Being a young company has also helped in curbing expenses. All the aircrafts are brand new A-320s. Apart from the fact that passengers get to fly in new aircrafts, these are also relatively much more fuel-efficient.

But Aditya doesn't want to save pennies at the cost of causing discomfort to IndiGo's passengers. Most of the low-cost carriers over the world have just two-and-a-half feet of space between the rows of seats. In India, the average height of men is lesser than that in the US and Europe. So adhering to the global standard allows him a little more legroom.

These are some reasons why passengers flock to IndiGo. 'As per August [2014] data tracked by India's airline regulator, the privately held carrier [IndiGo] that has carried 84 million passengers to date has a third of all domestic passengers... Media baron Kalanithi Maran's SpiceJet, lately a discount warrior, is a distant No. 2 with close to one-fifth share. Airline tycoon Naresh Goyal's 21-year-old Jet Airways, co-owned by Etihad

Airways, trails in the third spot,' reports *Forbes*.[2]

When IndiGo was launched, it was small fry, but with big ambitions. In 2005, IndiGo first hit the headlines at the Le Bourget air show in Paris. People hardly knew the brand, but it had placed an order of a hundred Airbus A-320s, whose delivery will be completed in 2015—one plane every month after the first eighteen months. In 2011, it signed another deal worth $15.6 billion to acquire 180 more aircrafts by 2025, starting in 2016, which means one new plane every twenty days.

Yet, Aditya will never spend a dime in vain, even for high-profile meetings. His actions reflect his airline's low-cost mantra. In November 2011, the heads of all the major airlines sought a meeting with the then Prime Minister Manmohan Singh to seek his help to tide over the crisis in the aviation industry. While the chiefs of other airlines came in premium chauffeur-driven cars, Aditya Ghosh and Rahul Bhatia reached the meeting in a CNG-fuelled Wagon R painted in the IndiGo colours. Aditya revealed to *The Economic Times* in 2012 that on the day of the meeting he had to choose between a Swift Dzire, a Winger and the Wagon R. 'The Winger and the Dzire are used to transport people within the airport. And so the Wagon R was available. It's a great car and it had [the] IndiGo colours.'[3] He is so cost-conscious that he doesn't even have a receptionist, or a corporate communications manager.

---

[2]Nazneen Karmali, 'How Rahul Bhatia Built InterGlobe and Its Airline IndiGo into a Class Act', *Forbes*, 24 September 2014.
[3]Binoy Prabhakar, 'How IndiGo's Aditya Ghosh Is the Only Airline Boss Still Flying', *The Economic Times*, 3 June 2012.

A mix of aviation books and management books adorn his bookshelf. Aditya also likes to read history. His father, a history lover, introduced him to the subject. 'For us to know who we are and where we are going, it is essential to remember where we came from,' says Aditya.

Aditya's inherent quality of not letting go of his roots has helped him stick to the initial promise made by IndiGo—good customer service at low cost. 'Be the very best that you can be, at everything you do, every day' is his motto.

Flying International

After conquering the domestic skies, it was time to look beyond India. Aditya knew it would not be easy. So he stuck to what IndiGo does best—low-cost flights for short distances that can be covered in four to five hours.

In 2011, IndiGo marked its foray into the international market by inaugurating flights from Bengaluru to Dubai. In the last two years, it has expanded to places such as Bangkok, Singapore, Muscat and Kathmandu. It is notable that when IndiGo charted its expansion plans, the domestic market was in a flux—Kingfisher Airlines owned by the flamboyant Vijay Mallya was out of business, and many others were shrinking their operations. And here was a company that was dreaming to step out of the country. Even after going international, it continued to be profitable. 'We broke even for the first time in March 2009. We have been profitable in each year since then,' Aditya told *Business Standard* in 2013[4].

Aditya is a risk-taker. Many who know him say that even if the international expansion had not worked, he would have had a Plan B. It was a business choice that he made at the time, and it did pay off well. The international market, he told *Business Standard* in the same interview, looked glamorous, but in India, with players closing shop, stagnating and cutting down operations, Aditya saw a better opportunity. The demand was increasing and capacity declining. Also, travel to nearby foreign destinations was increasing. He wanted a share in both.

Internationally, IndiGo has not gone on an expansion spree. In India as well, it flew to thirty-three destinations till 2013, while rivals flew anything between sixty and seventy. Aditya has ring-fenced the company in such a way that while moving up the ladder it doesn't slip.

'It is not important never to fail, but we must stand up each time we fall, dust ourselves off and start running all over again! (I had read something along these lines in a story in *Reader's Digest* as a teenager years ago and it has stayed with me ever since),' says Aditya, who doesn't mind taking a leap of faith at times.

While his professional life has soared, Aditya remains grounded as ever. For him, customer satisfaction takes precedence over everything else. 'Look at any feedback or criticism as a gift.

---

[4]Sudipto Dey, 'I Don't Lose Sleep Over AirAsia: Aditya Ghosh', *Business Standard*, 8 July 2013.

You can never bring joy to someone unless you understand their pain,' he says.

Even though IndiGo is the uncrowned hero of the Indian skies, with its sights on the horizon, Aditya knows he will have to continuously strive to pull down cost yet improve quality in order to survive. But for him, the airlines business is like a marathon, a long-term play.

ADITYA GHOSH'S MANTRAS FOR SUCCESS

There is a fundamental difference between the 'best of our efforts' and the 'best of our ability'. [...] we realize our true potential...things that we can do to the best of our ability, only once in a while. Therefore it is important to strive to the 'best of our ability' and not just to the 'best of our efforts'.

Never let ego come in the way of wisdom
(I feel this is particularly important for young leaders who often make the mistake of believing that they are 'in charge'!)

We should never be shy of thinking of, and thanking, all those [...] because of whom we can be the heroes that we are.

For us to know who we are and where we are going, it is essential to remember where we came from.

Be the very best that you can be,
at everything you do, every day.

It is not important never to fail, but we must stand up each time we fall, dust ourselves off and start running all over again!

Look at any feedback or criticism as a gift. You can never bring joy to someone unless you understand their pain.

ATUL SINGH

Atul Singh has been the group president, Asia Pacific, of the Coca-Cola Company since 2013, previous to which he was heading the India operations of Coca-Cola. Currently, he oversees the operations of thirty-six markets, including India. He is also a director on the Bata international board. He has chaired several committees on water, sports, environment, rural development and corporate social responsibility for the Federation of Indian Chambers of Commerce and Industry (FICCI) and the Confederation of Indian Industry (CII).

GETTING THE FIZZ BACK

Atul Singh inherited a company full of problems but slowly turned it around. Today, he has become one of Coca-Cola's most important faces globally.

In December 2003, the Centre for Science and Environment alleged that twelve brands including Coca-Cola and Pepsi contained pesticides beyond the allowed limit. The pesticide controversy plummeted Coca-Cola's sales within no time. Coca-Cola was also in a battle with the village panchayat of Plachimada in the Palakkad district of Kerala. The panchayat had complained that due to excessive extraction of water by the Coca-Cola bottling plant in the neighbourhood, there was a depletion of the water level and the water had got contaminated.

To make matters worse, the then country head, Sanjiv Gupta, quit because of differences with the management. The Indian subsidiary, which was the best performer globally for three consecutive years till the controversies, became financially weak. Amidst this turmoil, Atul Singh took charge as the deputy president of Coca-Cola India.

In a quarterly results press conference in Atlanta, USA, in June 2005, the company's global head said they did not expect much progress in India. Sales had gone down and the company was finding it difficult to cover the raw material and distribution costs.

This was Atul's second innings at Coca-Cola India. He was brought back to India to stabilize the business, or rather, to get the company out of the crisis. Atul had joined the company in 1998 as vice president, operations, of the India division. From 1998 to 2001, he headed the franchise operations and key accounts after which he became the company's president of the east, central and south China divisions. Before Coca-Cola, Atul had worked with Colgate-Palmolive, in three countries, for ten years. He had also worked with the global audit and consultancy firm PricewaterhouseCoopers, in New York.

The first thing he had to get right in the company was the financial performance. During Atul's earlier stint, Sanjiv Gupta had launched the iconic ₹5 Coke bottle. It was revolutionary, and factories had worked overtime pumping out these mini bottles. In fact, it had also captured the tea drinkers' market, due to its extremely cheap rate. Even though Coca-Cola subsidized these low-cost Coca-Cola bottles, it did the trick. They regained consumer confidence. Soon, Coca-Cola's competitors had also launched their versions of these chhota bottles.

Atul decided to go for an up to 60 per cent price hike in the price of this bestseller. 'There was no silver bullet. We had to restore financial health, and we knew it would be at the cost of a hit on volumes (sales),' he told *Business Today* in May

2009.[1] The chhota bottle was soon discontinued by Coca-Cola, but it had done its job.

Over the next few months, on the one hand, Atul successfully defended the pesticide taint in courts, and on the other, he stopped the product that had become a hit. He believes, 'It is important to have the courage to do the right thing, always. There will be occasions which will need bold but virtuous decisions. A leader should not shy away from taking the decisions that are right for the organization and right for the society at large, even if they turn out to be unpopular decisions.'

Thumbs Up for Thums Up

For the next three quarters, after taking the chhota bottle off the shelves, the company continued to make losses. It was during this time that Pepsi became India's top cola brand by displacing Thums Up from its top position. The reasons were not difficult to understand. Coca-Cola, which had acquired Thums Up, along with Gold Spot, Citra and Limca, in 1993 from the Parle group reportedly for $40 million, had started promoting the Coke brand as the flagship product. Atul soon realized that Thums Up's success was important for the company.

None of Atul's predecessors were able to manage the Thums Up portfolio like he did. On the contrary, Thums Up's value had been undermined, which benefited Pepsi rather than Coca-Cola. Thums Up started slipping from its position of the leading

---

[1] Shamni Pande, 'The Fizz Is Back', *Business Today*, 31 May 2009.

cola drink. Atul decided to use Thums Up as a weapon to attack Pepsi. And soon enough, in 2007, Thums Up regained its peak position.

Sprite Sprints Ahead

Sprite was introduced in India in 1999. The drink was targeted at the most lucrative segment of the market—the youth. The Sprite ambassador has always been the teenager himself—confident, smart and spontaneous. In 2006, the brand which had shunned celebrity endorsements till then, signed on a celebrity, Sania Mirza, the first mainstream female sports star in India. Taking a dig at advertising that mostly shows people acquiring super powers after having their products, Sprite got Sania to bust such pretences by revealing that she only drinks Sprite to quench her thirst—nothing more, nothing less.

By 2008, Sprite emerged as the number two drink in the sparkling beverage market in India. Then, in 2013, Sprite finally became India's numero uno sparking beverage brand.

Ten-year Plans

When Atul rejoined Coca-Cola India, he planned their strategy and operations till 2015. 'I have always set myself a ten-year vision map, both at a personal level and on the work front. I have done this when I was at the start of my career, managing a few clients, and I do this today, when I manage some of the largest Coca-Cola markets, in terms of volume,' he says.

Atul and his team documented their ten-year goals on a piece of paper and went about pursuing them in an organized, well-laid-out manner. Over the next ten years, he broke the vision into small steps or created milestones. 'This vision document included our aspiration to be one of the most respected companies in India. Today, we are the second-most respected FMCG company in India and that is an achievement, given our tumultuous journey in India,' he says.

At the same time, he wanted to measure the growth and progress of the vision. According to him, 'It is not just important to know where we want to be, it is equally important to know how we are going to get there.'

There were two things Atul did—one was expanding into rural India and the second was growing the company's portfolio beyond aerated drinks. Today, Coca-Cola India has nineteen brands, such as Diet Coke, Sprite, Limca, Fanta, Maaza, Minute Maid and Kinley, which includes aerated drinks, juices and water.

2010 turned out to be an important year. The company roped in Sachin Tendulkar, then the country's highest-paid brand endorser from the field of sports, to endorse Coca-Cola. This choice also reflects Atul's passion for cricket (he still has memories of the India-Australia cricket match he had seen at Eden Gardens, Calcutta, in 1969). As does the fact that Coca-Cola sponsored the Indian Premier League (IPL) team Kolkata Knight Riders in 2009, and their drink Sprite became the official team beverage.

Coca-Cola's association with these teams and sportspersons shows Atul's affinity towards sports, a childhood passion which still continues. Like in sports, Atul emphasizes the importance of teamwork in corporate circles, giving the example of another game he loves—football. 'It takes eleven players to score a goal and play the full ninety minutes of a football game. Business, too, requires teamwork. A successful leader must build a team, empower the team, sell them the larger organizational vision and then enable them to achieve their own goals and that of the organization.'

Atul grew up in Calcutta, studied at St Xavier's College and supported West Bengal's Mohun Bagan football club. He remembers watching Pele, the football legend, when he visited Kolkata for an exhibition match. His childhood has also left him with a taste for Bengali food—he loves luchi and kosha mangsho (a mutton preparation).

Putting in the Big Bucks

In 2011, the company also decided to invest another $2 billion in the next five years, the equivalent of what the company had invested in the last eighteen years of its existence in India. The money would go towards achieving some ambitious targets Atul had set. He loves the challenges that a leader faces: 'Work becomes fun and an indulgence when one enjoys it. So once you have made a choice, enjoy the many challenges that a leadership role brings.'

One of the challenges he faced was growing the company's distribution and retail networks. He has planned to double the number of outlets where Coca-Cola brands were available to three million in the next five years. The second target was more difficult—to double its turnover in the country. After all, the Indian operations had overtaken South Africa's in 2010 and Atul was looking at a new milestone to achieve.

'We will use it [the investment] to expand our bottling plants, set up more plants [Coca-Cola already has fifty units], build cold-storage assets, expand our rural and urban distribution and our trucking strength,' said Atul to *Business Standard* in 2011.[2]

The same year, Atul tried out some innovative marketing and distribution techniques, as heavy rainfall was affecting the sale of soft drinks. He started looking at home and office consumption, since those would be less affected by seasonality. He also put more focus on supplying to movie halls, malls and eateries. The statistics were clear—about 40 per cent of Coca-Cola's beverages were consumed at home or in offices.

But in the case of powdered ice tea, the number was as steep as 90 per cent. In order to boost sales, Atul did the same things that Sanjiv Gupta had done with the chhota cola bottles. The company came out with small sachets of the powdered drinks and priced them below ₹5.

For its fruit-juice manufacturing, Coca-Cola India was importing the pulp from China, Brazil and Florida. Atul came up with a plan to reduce costs. Coca-Cola partnered with the renowned Indian irrigation giant, Jain Irrigation Systems Limited, and imported 10,000 orange saplings to set up orange plantations

---

[2] 'Coca-Cola to Invest $2 bn in India over Five Years', *Business Standard*, 15 November 2011.

Getting the Fizz Back

in India. 'Senior leaders must have the knack of picking up local insights and cultural sensitivities. As the world becomes a global village and access is no longer a challenge, senior leaders are expected to be able to supervise business operations across multiple geographies,' says Atul, who travels abroad through more than half of the year, yet does not lose his eye on India.

The next plan was to target villages. To this end, Coca-Cola launched Vitingo, an orange beverage with micronutrients, as a pilot in Orissa. It partnered with NGOs for production and distribution of the product. Atul plans to take it to Tamil Nadu as well.

In 2013, Coca-Cola announced an investment of $5 billion by 2020. One of the targets now is rural India, where there is lack of infrastructure. 'One big challenge is going to be our penetration into the rural market, given the infrastructure and the lack of power and electricity. We need our products to be served chilled. And that is a real issue. We sell to 2 to 2.5 million FMCG outlets, and there are over 5 million outlets. That is a big challenge. We are making big strides, but in the grocery channel, we don't have the higher penetration, even in big cities, because of chilling equipment,' Atul told *Business Standard* in April 2013.[3]

Coca-Cola manufactures more than 3,000 products globally, and Atul is always looking to bring in viable ones to India. There are also some local products developed by their R&D department, which has developed the Minute Maid Nimbu

---

[3]Surajit Das Gupta and Sounak Mitra, 'Our Big Challenge is Going to be the Rural Market: Atul Singh', *Business Standard*, 17 April 2013.

Fresh lemon drink independently in India.

Atul admits that he wouldn't be able to do this without the people in his company. His connect with employees and his ability to delegate authority has helped him a lot. He has even called back many Indians who were working with Coca-Cola in other countries. He has also broken the strict hierarchy established by his predecessors and has started meeting his colleagues for lunches or breakfasts in small groups to discuss their problems. 'Hire for attitude and train for competence. Also hire and retain the best available, even if that means that the subordinate is smarter than the leader. Align the objectives with the team and then empower them to go out there and achieve it' is his mantra.

Now Atul is the group president of Coca-Cola, Asia Pacific, which also includes China, Korea, India, Southwest Asia and countries from the Association of Southeast Asian Nations (ASEAN). China and India, put together, sell 10 per cent of Coca-Cola's global volumes.

'An organization is known by its leader,' says Atul. Of course, after so many years, it is very difficult to take Coca-Cola out of Atul, and Atul out of Coca-Cola. He was Coca-Cola's crisis manager, and is now its flag-bearer.

ATUL SINGH'S MANTRAS FOR SUCCESS

It is important to have the courage to do the right thing, always. There will be occasions which will need bold but virtuous decisions. A leader should not shy away from taking the decisions that are right for the organization and right for the society at large, even if they turn out to be unpopular decisions.

I have always set myself a ten-year vision map, both at a personal level and on the work front.

It is not just important to know where we want to be, it is equally important to know how we are going to get there.

It takes eleven players to score a goal and play the full ninety minutes of a football game. Business, too, requires teamwork. A successful leader must build a team, empower the team, sell them the larger organizational vision and then enable them to achieve their own goals and that of the organization.

Work becomes fun and an indulgence when one enjoys it. So once you have made a choice, enjoy the many challenges that a leadership role brings.

Senior leaders must have the knack of picking up local insights and cultural sensitivities.

Hire for attitude and train for competence. Also hire and retain the best available, even if that means that the subordinate is smarter than the leader. Align the objectives with the team and then empower them to go out there and achieve it.

ACKNOWLEDGEMENTS

I would like to thank:

Mom, my first teacher. My first memory of books is from when I was a toddler, when she would show me the children's encyclopaedia and I would identify the pictures.

Dad, who has supported all my decisions.

John Sir and Mala Bose, my teachers from Ranchi.

Rajeev Dubey at *Businessworld*, who taught me reporting.

Josey Puliyenthuruthel John and Suveen Sinha at *Business Today*, who spent days teaching me how to write a copy.

Deeti Ojha, who stood by me like a rock, especially during my college days.

Anurupa, my sister, who means the world to me.

Dibakar Ghosh, who had to put up with my deadline misses and crazy schedules. I couldn't have got a better editor.

—Sunny Sen